Quit Drinking

How to Go Alcohol-Free in 30 Days (or Less)

Jack Rivers

Free Newsletter

Health, longevity and lifestyle tips and advice

Sign up to get the exclusive e-newsletter,
sent out every week

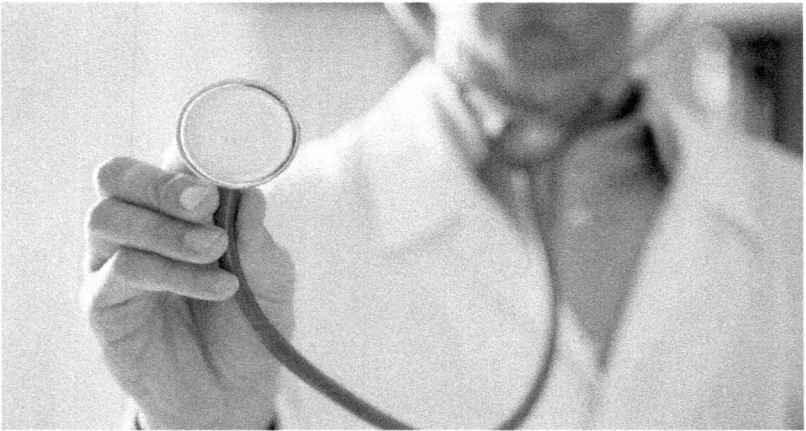

https://www.subscribepage.com/autoimmune

Table of Contents

Introduction

————◆◇◇◉◇◇◆————

There was no dramatic moment, no sudden realization that my life had shifted. It began quietly, with a shift in the background—first, a single glass of wine after a long day, a small indulgence to soften the edges of life's stress. Like so many others, my challenges with alcohol began with use that felt harmless, even comforting. I found relief in the way alcohol dulled my senses, feeling a temporary sense of calm wash over me, a temporary respite from the stress and chaos of the world. But over time, that simple act of having a casual drink or two grew into something I couldn't control. What started as a way to unwind became a struggle that consumed years of my life—a fight against something I never imagined would take hold of me.

I'm not sharing this to stand out, but to say that I am one of many. The truth is, I'm far from alone in this experience. Millions of people battle with alcohol every day. In fact, the National Institute on Alcohol Abuse and Alcoholism reports that over 28.9 million adults in the U.S. face alcohol use disorder annually (NIH, 2024), and an estimated

400 million people, or 7% of the world's population aged 15 years and older, live with alcohol use disorders (*Alcohol*, 2024). These aren't just numbers; and they are a quantified reflection of the many lives that are negatively impacted every single day by alcohol use, encompassing not just those who struggle with their consumption but their families, friends, and communities.

For so many, the story begins innocently enough— a toast at a party, drinks with colleagues, or perhaps a reward after a hard day. We tell ourselves that alcohol helps us relax, supports our social interactions, and takes the edge off of life's pressures. However, this is a deception so common that we barely notice that, in actuality, the substance that we think is easing our stress is actually amplifying it, wrapping us in a cycle that becomes harder to break with each passing day. The relief alcohol promises is fleeting, and it leaves behind heightened stress, anxiety, and dependence.

This book is for all of us—those navigating the rocky terrain of recovery, the silent supporters who stand by our sides, and the professionals dedicated to guiding us toward healing. You're about to embark on a journey that isn't just about breaking free from alcohol; it's about reclaiming your life and discovering the extraordinary potential within you to manage everything you thought you needed alcohol for on your own.

Inside, you'll find practical strategies designed to empower and uplift you as you rediscover life without alcohol. We delve into the realities of living sober and explore the emotional, physical, and mental transformations that accompany this journey. Through shared experiences, proven techniques, and expert guidance, you'll learn how to navigate challenges, celebrate victories, and carve out a vibrant, fulfilling life independent of alcohol's shadow.

To the friends and family members reading and considering sharing this book with someone who needs it: don't stop there. Your role is invaluable. Understanding what your loved one is experiencing can make all the difference, so please read along. You'll find tools and insights here to help you offer support with compassion and empathy while also addressing your own feelings and challenges along the way. Your strength, patience, and unwavering presence create a network of love and understanding that can make freedom from alcohol even more achievable.

Finally, for those uncertain about their relationship with alcohol, this is an opportunity to explore and reflect. Gaining clarity about drinking habits and seeking guidance for change is both brave and transformative. You, too, will find guidance within these pages, providing understanding and motivation to redefine your path moving forward by gaining insights and facts that can help you inform your relationship with alcohol with more knowledge and clarity. Most importantly, this is an invitation to reflect, explore, and take the first step—whether it's toward understanding, healing, or rebuilding. There's no single path, no perfect roadmap, but there is a way forward.

Let this be the starting point for revitalization, growth, and discovery. Welcome to a journey where the strongest version of yourself emerges, ready to shine, unshackled from alcohol's grip. Here's to new beginnings, transformative moments, and the beauty of a fully awake life. Together, we'll navigate this path, step by step, and move confidently into an alcohol-free future alive with promise and possibility.

Chapter 1:
The Alcohol Illusion—Why
You're Not the Problem

Alcohol has become so deeply woven into the fabric of our society that its presence often goes unquestioned. From casual happy hours to celebratory toasts, it is presented as a staple of relaxation, success, and connection. This normalization makes it easy to be unaware of the subtle ways alcohol impacts our well-being. Understanding the role of alcohol in our lives is a journey that can be both eye-opening and empowering. As we peel back the layers of its allure, the myth of alcohol as a panacea starts to unravel, and we gain insight into the less-discussed yet often far-reaching consequences of relying on alcohol.

In this chapter, we delve into the intricate ways society perpetuates the illusion that alcohol is essential for relaxation, celebration, and camaraderie. We will explore how societal norms and media representations influence our perceptions, leading many to equate alcohol with success and happiness. You will also gain insight into the many consequences of relying on alcohol as a coping mechanism—from heightened anxiety to physical dependency. By shedding light on these dynamics, the path toward breaking free from alcohol's deceptive hold becomes clear. Through alternative methods and healthier choices, you will discover avenues to promote genuine well-being and resilience. You will also gain insight into both the subtle and significant consequences of alcohol use, ranging from heightened anxiety to chronic illness.

The Reality Behind the Buzz

We live in a culture that seems to celebrate alcohol as a cure for all of life's challenges—a quick fix for stress, a balm for anxiety, and the spark for fun. Whether it's a glass of champagne to celebrate or a few cold beers after a long day, alcohol is often portrayed as useful for unwinding and socializing. But what if this belief is more myth than truth?

Let's unpack some of these beliefs, starting with the idea that alcohol alleviates stress. In fact, this belief seems to be one of the most common about alcohol and one of the most pervasive. We tend to hear about the negative side effects of overconsumption, but don't often question this particular myth. However, if we look at the actual data, contrary to this popular notion, alcohol isn't just ineffective in relieving stress, but it actually worsens anxiety over time. After the initial sense of relaxation from alcohol fades, individuals often experience heightened levels of stress and anxiety as a side effect, potentially creating an escalating cycle of dependency (Volkow et al., 2019).

Consider the example of Alex, a professional juggling a high-stress job and a busy family life. At the end of each day, Alex pours a glass of wine, telling himself it's a well-earned way to relax. Initially, it works—the wine takes the edge off, and Alex feels calmer, even momentarily lighter. But later that night, Alex finds himself restless, unable to sleep, and overwhelmed by racing thoughts. By morning, the stress feels even heavier. As the days go by, Alex not only begins to rely on that glass of wine as a nightly ritual, but decides to have an additional glass or two before bed, not realizing the temporary relief is only masking—and worsening—their anxiety. Over time, the single glass of wine each night has turned into three or four as Alex chases the fleeting sense of calm that alcohol initially provided. And, because it's been a gradual process, Alex is not fully aware that he's entered into a cycle of dependency.

The temporary illusion of anxiety relief and the accompanying cycle of dependency it creates can be subtle. Yet studies have consistently shown that such coping mechanisms only increase mental health issues, including anxiety and depression, exacerbating the very problems individuals attempt to escape (Koob, 2023). The immediate gratification often associated with alcohol masks its long-term detrimental effects on mental health. Although drinking may offer short-lived calmness, regular and excessive use can lead to serious consequences, including depression and addiction.

Alcohol's ability to diminish inhibitions and momentarily uplift mood stems from its impact on brain chemistry, particularly its effect on neurotransmitters like gamma-aminobutyric acid (GABA) and dopamine. When consumed, alcohol enhances GABA activity, producing a calming effect while simultaneously triggering a surge of dopamine, the brain's "reward" chemical, which creates feelings of pleasure and relaxation (Dresp-Langley, 2023). However, these effects are fleeting. As the body metabolizes alcohol, dopamine levels plummet, and the brain's natural balance is disrupted. This often leads to a rebound effect, where stress and anxiety return with greater intensity—a phenomenon sometimes referred to as "alcohol-induced anxiety" or "hangxiety" (Travers, 2024).

So, given this, why do societal narratives so frequently depict alcohol as a legitimate path to relief—a portrayal that traps individuals in cycles of perceived necessity and true reliance? A significant part of the answer lies in the powerful influence of the alcohol industry and its marketing strategies. Advertising campaigns and media representations glamorize drinking as synonymous with leisure, celebration, and sophistication, skillfully perpetuating myths about its role in enhancing life's joys. From commercials showcasing carefree gatherings over drinks to TV shows and movies that connect alcohol with moments of triumph or bonding, the industry carefully crafts narratives that equate drinking with happiness and success (Grube, 2024).

Media representations typically glamorize drinking while conveniently omitting the darker side of alcohol use, such as the challenges of withdrawal, the escalation of dependency, and the toll on mental and physical health. By focusing exclusively on the pleasures of drinking, the alcohol industry obscures its risks and deters many from exploring healthier, more sustainable coping mechanisms. This normalization of drinking continues to shape cultural expectations, making it difficult for individuals to critically evaluate their habits or recognize the harm embedded in habitual consumption. In this way, marketing doesn't just sell a product; it sells a lifestyle that prioritizes alcohol as essential, reinforcing a cycle that maintains the popularity of alcohol at the expense of personal and collective well-being toward

Breaking free from the misconceptions that have shaped our relationship with alcohol starts with acknowledging and understanding how it truly impacts our well-being. Genuine and long-term relief from stress and anxiety comes not from temporary numbing but from developing resilience and adopting healthy coping strategies. Individuals can move towards liberation from alcohol's hold by embracing practices such as mindfulness, exercise, or creative expression, which can replace unhealthy habits with nurturing ones and support a sense of empowerment and autonomy that can truly transform their lives. Support networks, including therapy and peer groups, offer guidance, encouragement, and a sense of community that can help individuals chart new paths toward wellness, free from the deceptive hold of alcohol.

The Many Ways Society Normalizes Drinking

While it would be easy to see through the illusion if alcohol's "benefits" were merely touted in advertisements and commercials, the reach of this false message extends much further. In contemporary society, alcohol isn't just something that is suggested in the media; it has become almost synonymous with socializing, deeply embedded in the fabric of many gatherings and celebrations. From family dinners to office parties to dating, the presence of alcoholic beverages is often assumed. At many social events, there is a tacit expectation for attendees to partake in drinking, crafting an environment where alcohol feels like an indispensable element of participation. The "strange behavior" of those who don't indulge is often viewed with a level of skepticism that can border on outright suspicion. For those navigating recovery or exploring sobriety, this can be particularly challenging, as opting out of drinking might feel synonymous with opting out of social engagement or, at the very least, answering unwelcome questions about their choice to abstain.

Of course, media representation significantly bolsters this perception by glamorizing alcohol consumption. Movies and TV shows often depict drinking as an essential element for enjoyment, humor, and sophistication, creating a compelling narrative about alcohol's role in enhancing social interactions. In countless films and series, characters are shown unwinding with a glass of wine after a long day, laughing over beers with friends, or celebrating success with champagne. Socially, many of these shows frequently depict bars as the central hub of interaction, where friendships are sustained over drinks. Similarly, advertisements romanticize alcohol by presenting idyllic scenes—a group of friends clinking glasses on a sunlit terrace or a sophisticated individual savoring a fine whiskey in an upscale lounge.

These portrayals craft an alluring narrative that positions alcohol as a magic conduit for memorable experiences while conveniently omitting its downsides. As we consume these ideas, we also start unconsciously equating alcohol with positive social outcomes, which further reinforces its appeal and usage, and it becomes cyclical in nature. The pervasive nature of alcohol in media shapes societal norms and individual attitudes toward drinking, impacting real-life behaviors and choices, and those choices then influence media portrayals. By setting unrealistic standards and consciously or subconsciously glorifying consumption, we end up with a culture where alcohol is not just normalized but casually celebrated without an honest depiction of its potential consequences.

This alcohol mythology permeates personal circles through peer pressure from friends and colleagues. In both professional settings and friendly meetups, individuals might find themselves nudged toward drinking, whether subtly or overtly. Happy hours can be seen as opportunities to bond with colleagues, creating an unspoken expectation to participate. Invitations to share a drink often can be positioned as a marker of connection and belonging. While some may genuinely enjoy these moments, others might comply simply to avoid feeling excluded or to fit in with the group, and often, the line between genuine desire and social obligation becomes so blurred over time that we aren't fully aware of why we are partaking, to begin with. This subtle yet persistent pressure can effectively undermine personal choices, making it difficult for those wanting to abstain to maintain their resolve. For example, someone who declines a drink might face teasing remarks like, "Come on, just one won't hurt," or feel the weight of raised eyebrows when choosing a non-alcoholic option. These social dynamics can create an environment where abstaining feels strangely like an act of social defiance rather than what should be a personal decision.

Cultural rituals and celebrations also complicate the journey for those considering sobriety. Weddings with champagne toasts, holidays marked by specific alcoholic traditions, and festivals abundant with crafted brews frequently place alcohol at the center of social bonding. For individuals who prefer not to drink, these settings can not only pose difficulties, they often further support the myth that alcohol consumption is the norm and sobriety is strange and out of place rather than an incredibly beneficial choice for both mental and physical health. Strangely, it has come to be regarded as almost a collective decision to dictate whether one should or should not drink rather than as a personal choice.

Set Yourself Free

As we clear up the myths surrounding alcohol, it's essential to recognize that there is a plethora of scientific data and research to back the idea that it's not the stress-buster or social enhancer it's often made out to be. Rather, alcohol is more often a deceptive trap that lures individuals with promises of relaxation and connection, only to deepen stress and anxiety in the long run, as well as contribute to other potential challenges we'll explore in more depth in the following chapters. By both understanding the roots of these alcohol myths and recognizing their inaccuracy, those on their journey to sobriety can begin to free themselves from the illusion and seek healthier, more fulfilling behaviors.

Imagine a life where joy comes from activities that truly nourish both body and soul—whether through the rush of physical movement in sports, the flow of creativity in artistic pursuits, or the warmth of deep, genuine connections, all without the risk of harmful side effects tied to drinking. Becoming aware of the societal norms that glorify alcohol is essential not just for those questioning their relationship with drinking, but for all of us who seek to live authentically. Whether you're navigating recovery, supporting a loved one, or simply examining your own habits, understanding the pervasive influence of media and peer pressure empowers you to make more informed choices that truly match your values and can open doors to greater possibilities for happiness, health and connection.

Chapter 2:
The 30-Day Challenge—What You'll Achieve

Imagine quitting alcohol as hitting the reset button on your life—not a punishment or deprivation, but an opportunity to rediscover a more energized and authentic version of yourself. In that sense, committing to 30 days without alcohol is more than just a temporary challenge; it's an invitation to step back, reflect, and explore what lies beneath the surface of your daily habits.

For many, alcohol is deeply embedded into routines, celebrations, and even coping mechanisms. But what happens when you set it aside? In just 30 days, the shifts in your life can be profound, revealing new levels of energy, physical health, and mental clarity. This challenge isn't just about what you're giving up—it's about embracing the benefits waiting to unfold. As the days pass, the fog alcohol often casts over the mind begins to lift, paving the way for sharper focus and a renewed sense of vitality. Emotional insights surface, offering clarity about feelings alcohol might have dulled or distorted. Unexpected joys emerge, too—a brighter complexion, improved sleep, and even a boost in financial well-being as your spending habits change can be some of the unexpected perks of quitting drinking.

This chapter isn't merely a guide for surviving the first 30 days without alcohol; it's an overview of what you stand to gain and how to stay motivated. From the practical strategies to keep you motivated to the deeper insights into how this choice can ripple into every corner of your life, you'll find yourself equipped with tools to embrace the challenge and celebrate its rewards. Whether your goal is a permanent lifestyle change or simply a chance to hit pause and reassess, this journey offers something invaluable: the chance to reconnect with your most authentic self. With each passing day, you'll see that it's not just about giving something up—it's about discovering everything you stand to gain.

What You'll Gain in 30 Days

As you step away from alcohol, a ripple effect occurs, setting off a momentum for positive change. The benefits will be nearly immediate, both physical, mental, and emotional, and continue to evolve as your body becomes free of toxins and full of energy. The following provides a more in-depth look at the benefits you'll experience in your first month of sobriety.

Physical Benefits

One of the most straightforward benefits of alcohol cessation is observed in physical health. While it may seem that this shift will take time, some of the physical benefits of quitting alcohol are nearly immediate and quite impactful. For example, consider nutrition and weight. By removing alcohol from your lifestyle, you indirectly reduce the unnecessary intake of empty calories. Not only are alcoholic drinks often surprisingly high in calories and potentially contributing to weight gain, but their consumption also tends to replace calories that contain nutrition (Wandler, 2024). When you consider that some alcoholic beverages contain as many calories as a full meal, consistently cutting out these calories can lead to effortless weight loss. For those who aren't experiencing issues with weight gain, eliminating alcohol can lead to the consumption of nutrient-dense foods that replace these empty calories, thereby increasing energy and well-being (Julius, 2024).

Not only is alcohol use associated with the consumption of empty calories, but it also has a significant impact on metabolic function, often slowing down the body's ability to efficiently process nutrients and maintain overall energy levels. For example, when you consume alcohol, your liver prioritizes metabolizing it over other essential functions, as alcohol is perceived as a toxin that needs immediate attention (Sharp, 2024). This diversion can hinder the breakdown of fats, carbohydrates, and proteins, leading to sluggish digestion and reduced nutrient absorption. Additionally, alcohol disrupts hormone regulation, particularly in hormones involved in appetite control and fat storage, which can contribute to weight gain and metabolic imbalances over time (Wandler, 2024). By removing alcohol from your routine, your body's natural metabolic processes are given the opportunity to function optimally, leading to improved digestion, better energy management, and enhanced physical health overall.

The healing does not just occur from the inside out. Quitting alcohol can have a transformative effect on your appearance, especially regarding your skin. Alcohol dehydrates the skin, dulls its natural glow, and weakens its elasticity, often leading to dryness, puffiness, redness, and premature aging (Julius, 2024). Over time, regular drinking can further exacerbate these issues, contributing to chronic dark circles, a blotchy complexion, and a tired, worn-out look. However, once you eliminate alcohol, your skin begins to recover, regaining moisture and vitality (Julius, 2024). You will likely notice a clearer complexion, reduced inflammation, and a more even skin tone. This improvement in your physical radiance can enhance self-confidence, as the changes resulting from quitting alcohol are reflected in a healthy glow.

You're also less likely to get sick or catch that bug going around the office soon after you quit drinking. Alcohol has a rapid impact on the immune system, weakening its ability to protect the body against illness and infection. Regular alcohol consumption disrupts the production and function of white blood cells, which are essential for fighting off pathogens (Ballard, 1997). It also hampers the gut's ability to maintain a healthy balance, a critical component of immune health (Bishehsari, et al., 2017). This compromised immunity can lead to increased susceptibility to colds, respiratory infections, and even slower recovery from wounds. As soon as you quit drinking, your body begins to rebuild its natural defenses, allowing the immune system to function more efficiently.

Mental Benefits

The mental clarity gained from sobriety is another shift that can occur quite rapidly. Alcohol consumption often results in a mental haze, clouding judgment, impairing short and long-term memory, and affecting concentration (Koob, 2023). These effects can occur long after alcohol is consumed, often the entire day following. Over time, chronic drinking can even reduce the volume of gray and white matter in the brain, which is critical for processing information and maintaining mental sharpness. However, when you quit drinking, your brain begins to recover. Studies indicate that within days or weeks of sobriety, neurochemical activity stabilizes, and cognitive performance improves (Volkow et al., 2019). The lifting of this "mental fog" not only enhances memory and focus, but also restores your ability to think clearly and make sound decisions, leading to a sense of mental rejuvenation. This renewed mental clarity can also support a greater level of personal and professional growth, offering a foundation for both making confident decisions and boosting productivity.

Emotional Benefits

Emotional balance is another significant benefit of quitting alcohol. While often used as a temporary coping mechanism, alcohol disrupts the delicate balance of neurotransmitters like serotonin and dopamine, which play critical roles in regulating mood (Rydzewska et al., 2023). Initially, alcohol can produce feelings of euphoria or relaxation by artificially boosting these chemicals. However, as its effects wear off, levels plummet, often leaving individuals prone to heightened anxiety, depression, irritability, or anger. This cycle of artificial highs and subsequent lows creates a feedback loop of emotional instability. Sobriety, on the other hand, brings about improved emotional regulation. Research shows that within weeks of quitting alcohol, the brain begins to restore normal serotonin and dopamine production, resulting in more consistent mood regulation (Rydzewska et al., 2023). This neurochemical stabilization enhances emotional resilience, enabling those who quit drinking to better understand and manage their feelings.

Financial Benefits

Beyond physical, mental, and emotional health improvements, quitting alcohol can offer substantial financial gains. The cost of purchasing alcoholic beverages, while sometimes overlooked, can accumulate significantly (Hassan et al., 2021). Cutting these expenses can free up significant funds, even in a short time. In the first 30 days of giving up drinking, these savings can be redirected toward healthier alternatives, such as nourishing groceries, gym memberships, or wellness classes, offering a double benefit of better health and financial empowerment.

In addition to direct spending on alcohol itself, avoiding alcohol reduces the risk of unexpected expenses related to alcohol use, such as late-night food runs, rideshare costs, or even damages from accidents caused by impaired judgment. Within the first month, individuals often notice a financial gain, allowing them to invest in meaningful experiences, build a safety net, or treat themselves to items or activities that enhance their quality of life—choices that bring immediate and tangible rewards.

Staying Motivated

During the first 30 days of sobriety, it's important to stay connected to the positive changes happening in your life, and one of the most effective ways to do so is through a blend of tracking and witnessing progress. By observing how you feel and noting key shifts, you can stay motivated while also seeing the tangible benefits of your decision to quit drinking. Tracking progress in a log or journal in recovery is an invaluable strategy.

It not only serves as a mirror reflecting your journey, but also keeps you grounded in reality, showing just how far you've come and where you still want to go. For example, by jotting down daily feelings and reactions, you can start to identify specific triggers that may lead to cravings or emotional turmoil, but you can also get an opportunity to notice gradual positive shifts in your mental and physical wellness (Julius, 2024).

Additionally, consider logging trends in emotional and physical states, such as changes in energy levels, mood stability, or improvements in your appearance. Whether through a quick journal entry, a mobile app, or simply a mental note, documenting these changes allows you to track how your body and mind are responding to sobriety. You are more likely to notice a clearer mind, less emotional reactivity, and increased physical vitality if you keep track of these states daily. Eventually, this log can serve as a powerful reminder of how far you've come. As your body adjusts to a new lifestyle, you'll likely notice fluctuations in energy, often trending positively as health improves. Seeing proof that what you do every day impacts how you feel is motivating and can propel you further along your journey.

Additionally, observing immediate benefits, such as improved skin clarity or having more money available for meaningful purchases or experiences, provides concrete evidence of your success. Reflecting on these changes gives you a deeper appreciation for the positive transformations that sobriety brings. If weight loss motivates you, you may consider incorporating weigh-ins or measurements, which can be quantifiable reminders of your progress.

While what motivates you is likely unique and personal, keeping track of each small milestone achieved reinforces your dedication to sobriety and can inspire your continued efforts in maintaining it. To make these tracking practices most effective, it's important to find methods that suit your personality and lifestyle. Whether through traditional journaling, mobile apps, or simple spreadsheets, the key is consistency. Regular entries allow you to reflect back and analyze trends over time, offering a richer understanding of your personal journey.

Ultimately, the goal is not just to track progress, but to witness your own transformation. Each milestone, whether big or small, deserves recognition, reinforcing your commitment and determination. As you track these subtle shifts and witness your growth, you'll find yourself more motivated to continue the journey, knowing that each day without alcohol brings you closer to a healthier, more vibrant version of yourself. You'll also have a record of these 30 days that might prove to be quite nostalgic a year from now if you've continued on the alcohol-free path and see a dramatic change in your life.

You're on Your Way to a New Life

As you embark on this 30-day journey of alcohol-free living, you'll experience many shifts in your life. Your body will adjust to healthier choices, and you'll see noticeable improvements—such as weight loss, glowing skin, and increased energy. However, the impact goes deeper. Freed from the fog of regular drinking, your mind will clear, sharpening your decision-making and allowing you to focus on what truly matters.

As you move through these first days, keep in mind that sobriety is more than just abstaining from alcohol; it's about embracing a new way of living that prioritizes well-being and self-awareness. Every small victory deserves recognition, as it all contributes to the larger picture of transformation. Remember, while quitting drinking can have rapid positive impacts, it isn't a race; it's a process in which the journey of experiencing your increasing wellness day by day makes the experience richer. As you reflect on the progress you've made, let these insights guide you toward a future full of possibility, where every alcohol-free day opens the door to further growth and renewal.

Chapter 3:
Rewiring Your Brain—How Alcohol Hijacks You

—————— ✦◇◇◉◇◇✦ ——————

Breaking free from alcohol's grip starts with understanding the powerful influence it has on your brain and your life. Alcohol doesn't just alter your mood; it taps into your brain's reward system, creating a cycle that is hard to break. Rewiring your brain is all about understanding the intricate dance between alcohol and your neural pathways. But knowing this is just the start of how you can take back control. When alcohol floods your brain with dopamine, it creates an artificial sense of euphoria that makes you crave more. This isn't simply a bad habit, but a deeply embedded pattern that intertwines with your natural desires for pleasure and reward. The challenge lies not just in resisting the urge to drink but in recognizing these cravings for what they are—a chemical reaction manipulated by alcohol. In this chapter, we'll delve into the science behind how alcohol manipulates your brain's wiring, hijacking your reward circuits and making it difficult to stop drinking. We'll explore how dopamine and habit loops come into play in this process. By leveraging neuroplasticity, the brain's ability to adapt and change, it's not only possible to pave new, healthier pathways, but quitting alcohol could help you develop a healthier state of mind than you had before you began.

The Science of Dopamine and Habit Loops

At the heart of alcohol's impact on the brain lies dopamine, a neurotransmitter that plays a central role in our experience of pleasure, as well as being associated with addiction. Dopamine is integral to the brain's reward system and is typically released in response to fulfilling essential needs or achieving pleasurable experiences, including essential tasks such as eating or exercising, as well as engaging in enjoyable social interactions. When we experience something rewarding, dopamine neurons fire, sending signals that promote feelings of happiness and satisfaction (Dresp-Langley, 2023).

The biological function of dopamine is to motivate us to pursue activities that benefit our well-being. For example, in early humans, dopamine was linked to motivation to forage, driving us to gather fruit and plants that activated this reward chemical, a necessary process to compel early humans to seek nourishment (Koob, 2023). However, alcohol consumption provides an artificial shortcut to this pleasure response by drastically increasing dopamine pathways in the brain. When alcohol enters the bloodstream, it stimulates the release of dopamine from the brain's reward pathways, especially in the nucleus accumbens, which is a crucial region associated with pleasure and reinforcement (Volkow et al., 2019).

This excess dopamine activation creates euphoric sensations, which can lead to repeated consumption as individuals seek to recreate those fleeting moments of joy. Over time, this can manifest as a cycle of cravings, where the body begins to rely on alcohol to achieve the same level of dopamine release, thereby increasing tolerance and the need for higher quantities of alcohol (Merrill & Thomas, 2013). This particular pattern of dopamine leads to dependence on not only alcohol but is the same neurobiological process that leads to addictions of all kinds.

The binge/intoxication stage highlights how deeply rooted these pathways can become. Here, the brain's reward circuits are engaged, linking pleasurable experiences with cues present during drinking. In this stage, drinking produces a flood of dopamine, reinforcing feelings of pleasure and relaxation. Over time, external cues—such as the clink of glasses, the buzz of social gatherings, or even the sight of a familiar bar—become inextricably linked to these pleasurable experiences. Over time, these cues themselves gain motivational significance, further entrenching the habit. This insight into brain circuitry underscores the importance of understanding and reshaping our interactions with alcohol-related environments.

Habit Loops

This manipulation of brain chemistry by alcohol not only can create a neurochemical dependence but also intersects significantly with how our mind forms habits. To fully understand this, we must first examine the concept of habit loops—a cycle consisting of three essential components: trigger, routine, and reward.

A trigger, also known as a cue, is any stimulus that initiates a behavior, or in this case, is the catalyst for the habit loop. This can be an external event, such as a social gathering or a certain time of day, or an internal factor, such as an emotional state, like stress or boredom. These triggers activate the brain's desire for a reward, setting off a chain reaction (Vazifehkhorani et al., 2022).

Next, the routine is the behavior we engage in following the trigger. In the context of alcohol consumption, the routine often involves reaching for a drink in response to the trigger. This behavior is not merely a choice but, over time, becomes a conditioned response ingrained in the brain through repeated reinforcement. As we engage in this routine repeatedly, it becomes increasingly automatic, requiring less conscious thought (Vazifehkhorani et al., 2022).

Finally, the reward is the external response combined with the internal neurochemical reaction received after completing the routine. In the case of drinking, the reward is the pleasurable feelings induced by dopamine release, which reinforces the behavior, further strengthening the habit This reward strengthens the association between the trigger and the routine, making it more likely that the cycle will repeat in the future, forming a habit loops (Vazifehkhorani et al., 2022).

Over time, these habit loops become more and more deeply embedded in our neural pathways, creating patterns that can not only be difficult to break but sometimes be almost unconscious. The brain essentially wires itself to expect the reward from the routine in response to specific triggers, and our behavior and responses become automatic and mostly no longer in our conscious control. This process influences not only daily behaviors but also long-term patterns of consumption, such as alcohol use.

Understanding habit loops is useful for individuals seeking to change their drinking patterns or any other habitual behavior. By recognizing the triggers that lead to the routine of drinking, people can begin to devise strategies to interrupt the cycle. Often, temporarily removing oneself from the trigger can give the brain space to rewire so a person can consciously form new habits. For instance, if certain social settings serve as a trigger, individuals might explore alternative activities or environments that don't involve alcohol as they are recovering. By disrupting the established habit loop and introducing healthier routines, individuals can gradually reshape their habits and reduce reliance on alcohol for the reward of pleasure.

Environmental cues play a significant role in reinforcing drinking habits. The places and situations we associate with alcohol consumption can subtly influence our behavior. A familiar bar, a friend who shares your drinking habits, or even passing a liquor store can serve as potent reminders of past drinking routines (Sudhinaraset et al., 2016). Altering these environmental factors becomes essential. Simple changes, such as rearranging living spaces, avoiding known drinking spots, or seeking out new social circles, can help disrupt the automatic associations tied to alcohol. Creating a fresh environment can make it easier to resist the ingrained pull of old habits and support the development of new, positive ones.

Stress Responses During Recovery

When individuals quit consuming even moderate amounts of alcohol, they may face a hypodopaminergic state of withdrawal, where the absence of alcohol leads to decreased dopamine, diminished reward activity, and heightened stress responses (Merrill & Thomas, 2013). This challenging period is often what pushes people to return to drinking, as it often encompasses negative emotional states, making it tempting to return to alcohol use for temporary relief. Understanding this stage can prepare individuals for the challenges of withdrawal and emphasize the necessity of developing alternative coping mechanisms, as well as making efforts to reduce external stress as much as possible during the early stages of quitting alcohol.

The prefrontal cortex, the region of the brain that governs decision-making and impulse control, also can have impairments in the early stages of quitting drinking. These impairments, part of the impact of alcohol use over time, can manifest as strong urges to drink in response to stress and a lower ability to inhibit acting on those urges (Sharp, 2024). Recognizing the neurological underpinnings of these cravings can empower individuals to devise strategies that mitigate their impact, such as engaging in alternative activities or seeking community support to help face the strength of these urges.

Fortunately, many health and wellness professionals and support group leaders have knowledge of these neurological processes and incorporate them into treatment plans and support resources. Because of this, connecting with professionals or groups directly related to quitting drinking can help one discover stress management techniques and coping skills that are directly supported by the neuroscience of what alcohol does to the brain, providing invaluable support and a greater likelihood of long-term success.

Rewiring Your Brain to Crave Healthier Rewards

While dopamine is the base of addiction, when channeled properly, it serves as the brain's most powerful motivator that drives us toward achieving goals, building connections, and finding joy in life's pursuits.it is also as a whole. Cultivating healthy rewards is fundamental in overcoming alcohol dependency, as it shifts the focus from detrimental habits to positive, fulfilling experiences that apply dopamine to develop healthy habits.

The journey to developing healthier habits and reward systems in our brain begins by exploring activities that naturally boost dopamine levels—similar to how alcohol does, but without the harmful effects. Engaging in hobbies and social interactions offers benefits far beyond simple distractions. Activities like picking up a new craft, such as painting or gardening, not only can fill time but also stimulate the mind and provide a sense of accomplishment. Similarly, participating in sports, joining clubs, or attending community events fosters social connections and builds a support network essential for recovery (Dresp-Langley, 2023). These social interactions create a natural reward system that delivers joy, camaraderie, and a renewed zest for life.

Establishing personalized reward systems is key to maintaining motivation for sobriety. Celebrating progress, no matter how small, reinforces positive behavior, making it easier to stay the course. For example, setting achievable goals like remaining sober for a certain period, such as the holidays, or successfully managing stress without alcohol during an eventful time can be celebrated through healthy treats, a day trip, or taking time for something meaningful—anything that brings happiness or a sense of achievement. These celebrations also mentally link effort with reward, strengthening the resolve to continue (Volkow et al., 2019). Over time, this practice ensures that the pursuit of healthier rewards becomes habitual, gradually replacing the urge to seek alcohol for fulfillment.

Another method involves re-associating activities previously linked to alcohol with healthier alternatives. This helps rewire brain connections in a way that breaks the attachment to alcohol-fueled enjoyment. For instance, someone who associates weekend evenings with drinking might host non-alcoholic gatherings, watch movies, play games, or engage in meaningful conversations with friends instead. Over time, these new routines form neural pathways that foster healthy habits and diminish the power alcohol holds over emotional responses and cravings. This deliberate redirection of desires not only aids in physical recovery but also nurtures emotional well-being.

Community support is invaluable when transitioning to healthy rewards. Joining groups or attending meetings provides more than just accountability—it creates a space for shared experiences that reinforce the commitment to sobriety. Being surrounded by others who understand the journey can inspire confidence and provide encouragement during difficult times. Support groups also serve as a platform where successes are celebrated together and challenges are collectively addressed, making the path to recovery less daunting and more inclusive. Shared stories of triumph and resilience can reignite hope and motivation, reminding individuals that they are not alone on this road to sobriety.

Brain-Hacks to Overcome Cravings

Cravings can feel like an overwhelming tide, pulling individuals back into patterns they're striving to escape. But by implementing simple strategies that apply your knowledge of brain chemistry, more where the release of neurotransmitters like dopamine plays a significant role. When cravings arise, the brain's reward system is activated, releasing dopamine and inducing feelings of pleasure and satisfaction associated with past behaviors. However, by implementing simple strategies that apply your knowledge of brain chemistry, these cravings can be managed more effectively.

Deliberate Pauses

One of the most powerful techniques to harness this reward system in your favor is the 5-minute rule—a deliberate pause before reacting to cravings. This short but crucial interval allows the prefrontal cortex, responsible for decision-making and self-control, to dominate the emotional responses generated by the limbic system, where cravings originate. When a craving strikes, setting a timer for five minutes allows you to reflect on why you're feeling the urge without succumbing immediately. This pause gives the brain time to recalibrate, reducing the immediate chemical rush associated with the craving (Dresp-Langley, 2023).

During this interval, your mind can engage in a process of cognitive appraisal, assessing the craving's impact on long-term goals and health, thus empowering you to make more informed choices. Although it may sound trivial, it's a practical tool that provides the necessary space to consider healthier alternatives, disrupt automatic responses, and diminish the craving's hold over time (Koob, 2023). By understanding and leveraging the neurochemical mechanisms at play, individuals can regain control over their impulses and shift towards more positive behaviors.

Conscious Breathing

Incorporating mindful breathing exercises can also significantly support one's ability to mediate an alcohol-based reward system. Deep, conscious breathing acts like a reset button for your nervous system, allowing you to curb your response when cravings occur (Czepa, 2024). Specifically, by inhaling deeply through the nose, holding for a few seconds, and then exhaling slowly through the mouth, you send calming signals to your brain. These exercises not only help you navigate through intense moments, but also reinforce a behavior that can support emotional resilience in all stressful areas of your life. Over time, this practice builds a foundation of calmness and control, shifting how your body and mind respond to triggers to begin with (Volkow et al., 2019).

Written Reflection

Another supportive tool for managing cravings is journaling. Writing down thoughts and feelings related to your experiences with alcohol can not only allow you to increase your awareness at the moment, it can offer profound insights. Writing often helps identify recurring triggers—what happens right before the craving sets in serves as a mirror reflecting personal patterns and behaviors that might otherwise remain unnoticed—which can be highly supportive in adapting to manage these events. It can also help one to track progress over time. By logging these observations consistently, individuals can witness their journey toward sobriety with far more clarity and self-awareness and a better understanding of their own motivations and challenges, which is useful for long-term recovery.

Distractions Are Okay—but Mindfulness Is Key

While mindful journaling and self-awareness are valuable tools, it's important to acknowledge that during moments of intense cravings, the need for distractions is natural and should not be judged. Equally important, however, is ensuring that distractions are chosen consciously to avoid replacing alcohol addiction with new dependencies or maladaptive behaviors.

Redirecting focus to engaging activities can provide a powerful antidote to cravings, whether it's diving into a creative pursuit like painting or music or something physical like gardening or cycling. When selected thoughtfully, these activities offer a healthy outlet for the energy that might otherwise feed the craving. They also help rewire the brain to associate pleasure with positive stimuli, gradually fostering healthier behavioral patterns.

It's essential, however, to strike a balance. Activities that provide distraction should enhance your well-being rather than serve as a crutch or escape. For instance, while gaming, shopping, or excessive screen time might temporarily alleviate cravings, over-reliance on these activities can lead to new habits that are equally detrimental to mental or emotional health.

Here's where understanding your preferences and limits becomes crucial. Different distractions work for different people based on their interests and needs. Some find solace in artistic expression, while others prefer kinetic activities or social interactions. Building a repertoire of diverse options ensures flexibility and reduces the risk of falling into boredom or unhealthy patterns. The goal is to engage in activities that not only divert attention but also contribute to your overall growth and recovery. By approaching distractions mindfully and ensuring they align with your recovery goals, you can create a healthier, more balanced pathway to long-term sobriety.

Make It Personal

A significant part of successfully managing cravings involves developing personal strategies to apply these practices. For instance, practicing the 5-minute rule could mean setting specific intentions before starting the timer—reminding oneself of personal reasons for staying sober. With structured breathing exercises, following a guided pattern daily can enhance mindfulness and strengthen the habit. Similarly, maintaining a structured journal entry process helps capture essential details consistently, providing richer data for reflection. Meanwhile, creating a personalized distraction toolkit with one's favorite activities can ensure readiness at any time to curb a craving. By equipping themselves with these tools, individuals recovering from alcoholism can rewrite their narratives, focusing on strengths rather than struggles (Chiasson, 2025).

It's also important to remember that while each of these methods greatly aids in managing cravings, they work best when integrated into a larger recovery plan. Seeking community support, professional guidance, or attending group sessions can complement these strategies, offering additional layers of accountability and encouragement.

Reflections

Alcohol's manipulation of the brain's reward system can be elusive, especially in how it hijacks our body's natural reward system. By understanding how alcohol artificially inflates dopamine levels to create cravings and urges, we see how habitual drinking patterns are formed and reinforced. Fortunately, simple strategies, like identifying stressors and replacing habitual responses with healthier alternatives, can aid in rewiring our brains away from the reliance on alcohol for pleasure or relief. As you navigate your alcohol-free journey, remember that with awareness and intentional changes, it's possible to reclaim control and design a fulfilling life that doesn't rely on drinking.

Chapter 4:
Week 1—the Detox Phase

❖◇◇◉◇◇❖

The detoxification process begins the moment you stop drinking, with the first week of sobriety often being the most intense as a result. This initial phase, especially for those who drink frequently or heavily, can feel like an uphill battle, marked by difficult shifts in both body and mind. Yet, these shifts often bring discomfort—physical sensations and emotional turbulence that, without preparation, may tempt some to revert to old habits.

However, with determination, within these challenges are the seeds of change—the beginnings of a process that promises healing and renewal. In this chapter, we'll explore the physical and emotional symptoms that accompany detoxification in more detail, which can help to set expectations and prepare for some of the more challenging effects. Moreover, you'll gain an understanding of the emotional rollercoaster that might ensue so you can better prepare for mood swings, irritability, and anxiety, which are often companions while detoxing from alcohol. Armed with practical tips and knowledge, you'll be better equipped to navigate your first week of sobriety with both determination and self-compassion.

Understanding Physical and Emotional Detox Symptoms

The journey of recovery from alcohol dependency is a path filled with opportunities for growth, particularly during the transformative first week of detoxification. However, it is not without challenges and is often marked by severe withdrawal. Understanding both the physical and emotional symptoms that occur during this phase can equip individuals with the awareness needed to persevere through discomfort, recognizing it as an integral part of the healing process. It is advantageous to acknowledge that the body and mind react distinctly to the sudden absence of alcohol, manifesting various symptoms that can be daunting yet temporary.

Physical Symptoms

The body's response to eliminating alcohol presents itself through several physical symptoms. Headaches, fatigue, and changes in appetite are common indicators of the body adjusting to a new equilibrium without alcohol interference. These manifestations result from the body's attempt to rebalance neurotransmitter levels, which alcohol previously altered. The following conditions may occur as a result of the detoxification process.

Headaches

Headaches are a prevalent and often debilitating physical symptom experienced during the process of alcohol detoxification. These headaches result from a significant physiological response as the body begins to adjust to the absence of alcohol, which has typically constricted blood vessels in the brain. Once alcohol consumption stops, these blood vessels undergo a process of expansion, leading to increased blood flow and pressure in the cranial area (Sachdev, 2023). This sudden vascular adjustment can cause tension, tightening sensation, and discomfort, often presenting as throbbing pain. While the intensity and frequency of these headaches may vary from individual to individual, they generally subside as the body gradually adapts to the new normal of functioning without alcohol.

In addition to vascular changes, the role of neurotransmitters in this discomfort is critical. Alcohol influences the balance and regulation of neurotransmitters, including serotonin, which is known for its effect on mood and pain perception

QUIT DRINKING

(Sharp, 2024). During detox, the disruption of serotonin levels can amplify the intensity of headaches, making them feel more severe than typical tension or migraine headaches. The brain's altered chemical environment contributes to heightened sensitivity to pain, leaving individuals feeling more vulnerable to these distressing symptoms.

Fatigue

Another prevalent symptom is fatigue, as the body expends significant energy, restoring its natural chemical balance. The withdrawal process often triggers a cascade of physiological changes, including the restoration of natural neurotransmitter levels, the regeneration of liver and other organ cells, and the rebalancing of metabolic processes (Trevisan, 1998). These activities are energy-intensive, leaving individuals feeling physically and mentally drained. Sleep disturbances, such as insomnia or disrupted REM cycles, often accompany detox, compounding fatigue. Without alcohol's sedative effect, the body may struggle to achieve restful sleep, making recovery feel even more exhausting (Sharp, 2024).

48

Appetite Changes

Appetite fluctuations can range from increased hunger as the metabolism adjusts to decreased cravings due to withdrawal-related stress. Some individuals may experience heightened hunger, particularly for sugar-laden foods (Trevisan, 1998). This is because alcohol consumption disrupts blood sugar regulation, and the body may crave quick energy sources like sugar as it recalibrates. On the other hand, others might experience a loss of appetite due to stress, nausea, or general discomfort associated with withdrawal. These appetite fluctuations are the body's way of signaling its attempt to restore balance and heal.

Emotional Symptoms

In addition to physical challenges, the detox phase can evoke a range of emotional symptoms, mood swings, irritability, and heightened anxiety. Mood swings are partly due to the uneven production of dopamine and serotonin—neurotransmitters that regulate emotions- being significantly impacted by alcohol use (Sharp, 2024). When individuals consume alcohol, it often leads to artificially elevated levels of these chemicals, creating a temporary sense of well-being. However, during detox, as the body adjusts to the absence of alcohol, the production of these neurotransmitters can become erratic, resulting in rapid shifts in emotions. Individuals may experience a rollercoaster of feelings, ranging from intense anger to deep sadness and overwhelming frustration, mixed with temporary moments of relief, making emotions feel unpredictable and mental stability elusive.

Irritability and Sensory Overload

Irritability often emerges as a consequence of the body's struggle to cope without the sedative effects of alcohol. The brain becomes accustomed to the depressant influence of alcohol to manage stress and anxiety; thus, its absence can leave individuals feeling on edge and more easily triggered by stressors that they previously managed with a degree of numbness. The numbing effects of alcohol also tend to dull the senses, making sensory experiences seem more intense during detoxification. Without proper awareness or preparation, this heightened reactivity can manifest as combative behavior or emotional outbursts, complicating the early stages of quitting alcohol.

Anxiety and Panic Attacks

Anxiety is another common emotional challenge experienced during detox. As the nervous system recalibrates from the constant stimulation reciprocated through alcohol consumption, feelings of unease and apprehension become more pronounced (Koob, 2023). This heightened state of anxiety can disrupt daily functioning and lead to overwhelming feelings of dread or panic.

Panic attacks may also emerge during this period, characterized by sudden and intense surges of fear accompanied by physical symptoms such as palpitations, shortness of breath, shaking, and a sense of impending doom. As the body's systems adjust to the absence of alcohol, the likelihood of panic attacks may increase due to the brain's fluctuations in neurotransmitter levels, especially serotonin and gamma-aminobutyric acid (GABA), which are critical in regulating mood and anxiety (Volkow et al., 2019). These episodes can be particularly distressing, as they mimic the sensation of losing control or experiencing a heart attack, causing individuals to become even more fearful of their anxiety and the possible onset of future attacks. The experience of panic can feel disempowering and often compel individuals to seek immediate escape or relief, risking a relapse.

Detox Is Different For Everyone

Recognizing that each individual's experience of discomfort during detox is unique is key to alleviating feelings of inadequacy. Everyone's timeline for recovery can vary significantly based on factors like the duration and intensity of past drinking behaviors, overall health, and even genetic predispositions. One person's symptoms may subside within a few days, while another's may persist longer (Sharp, 2024). Remember, your journey through detox is uniquely yours, and every step forward is a victory worth celebrating. It's natural to feel uncertain when discomfort arises, but understanding that everyone's experience is different can help you replace self-doubt with self-compassion.

The path to an alcohol-free life doesn't follow a one-size-fits-all timeline. What matters most is embracing your progress and letting go of any pressure to meet an imagined standard of recovery. Your path is not meant to mirror anyone else's. By acknowledging this, you give yourself the grace to move at your own pace, with patience and courage as your guiding lights.

Finally, keep in mind that detox is a temporary experience. While symptoms such as headaches or anxiety may feel overwhelming at the moment, it is important to remember that they will not last forever. Most symptoms peak within the first 24-72 hours and gradually diminish as the body continues to adjust and heal (Trevisan, 1998). Maintaining this perspective can help you stay focused on your long-term goals of sobriety and wellness, knowing that every moment of discomfort is a step towards reclaiming control over your life. Celebrate small victories along the way, such as waking up clearer-minded or experiencing less severe symptoms, as part of a commitment to the recovery process.

Day-By-Day Survival Tips for the Detox Phase

As temporary as it is, it can still help to have strategies in place to handle some of the most challenging symptoms of the first week of quitting drinking. Keeping focused on these daily practices will also empower you to face each hurdle with resilience while maintaining motivation.

Before Day 1, it's useful to anticipate potential triggers that may jeopardize your commitment to sobriety. Triggers can vary greatly from person to person; they might be emotional states, such as stress or loneliness, specific environments, or even particular times of the day. Identifying these triggers before your detox symptoms begins allows you to consciously avoid them or develop coping mechanisms beforehand.

Preparing a support system is equally important at this stage. Share your goals with trusted family members or friends who can offer encouragement and accountability. Especially if you've faced challenges with quitting drinking in the past, it can also be beneficial to connect with a mentor or counselor specializing in addiction recovery who can guide you through the process and provide practical advice when challenges arise. Establishing this network not only strengthens personal accountability but also fosters a sense of community, reminding you that you are not alone in your journey.

By Day 2, focusing on hydration and nutrition can play a significant role in mitigating detox symptoms such as headaches and fatigue. As the body begins flushing out toxins from the body, proper hydration can aid in aiding cellular function and help keep this process in motion. Start each morning with a glass of water, and aim to consume around 3 to 4 liters throughout the day. Similarly, the healthier and more chemical-free your diet is during this time, the easier it will be for your body to focus on flushing out alcohol and detoxing effectively. Additionally, prioritizing balanced meals that incorporate lean proteins, fruits, vegetables, and whole grains helps replenish lost nutrients and stabilize blood sugar levels, which can support mood and energy.

As you'll potentially find yourself craving sugar and high-sodium foods, consider preparing your meals in advance to ensure healthy choices are readily available. This can significantly reduce the temptation to revert to less favorable eating habits, which are common in the detox phase. Simple swaps, like choosing water with fruit essence and honey over sugary artificial beverages or choosing crisp vegetables when you are craving chips or salty treats, can make a noticeable difference in how you feel and manage withdrawal effects.

As you move into Day 3, connections with others become increasingly important. Feelings of isolation as you shift from social routines that involve alcohol can heighten emotional distress, particularly during early recovery. Engaging with supportive friends or healthy communities not centered around drinking can provide both comfort and motivation. Regular interactions with peers who share similar goals or interests also afford you an outlet to express and discuss challenges candidly, making the path to sobriety feel less solitary.

From Days 4 to 7, you'll continue to maintain healthy nutrition and awareness of potential triggers, but you also can start slowly creating a new daily routine. Your symptoms are likely to be slowly decreasing, giving you the space to consider how you will replace old drinking habits with healthier activities. Routines also establish structure and predictability, which can counteract feelings of chaos often experienced during detoxification.

In that sense, it can help to begin each day on your alcohol-free journey with new rituals that promote wellness, such as stretching upon waking or engaging in mindfulness practices like meditation or journaling. These practices can set a positive tone and can significantly impact your mindset by promoting calmness and focus. Incorporating even small amounts of r physical activity when you wake up—whether it be jogging, yoga, or a brisk walk—can also boost endorphins that elevate mood and further help to ease the emotional challenges of moving forward.

Evening routines focused on winding down—such as reading, listening to relaxing music, or light stretches—promote restful sleep and ensure adequate recovery time for both body and mind. Additionally, carving out evening time for hobbies and interests previously overshadowed by alcohol use can provide fulfillment and occupy idle moments, reducing the risk of relapse.

Incorporating Mindset Exercises and Affirmations

In the early stages of recovery, the right mindset can significantly impact your journey toward sobriety. Mindset exercises and affirmations are beneficial tools in this transformative process and can help you be intentional about your emotional processes surrounding your alcohol-free journey.

Starting each day with motivating and positive affirmations can set a supportive tone for the rest of the day and significantly enhance emotional well-being during challenging periods like detox. By intentionally focusing on uplifting statements, you also construct a mental framework that helps shift your perspective toward growth. Affirmations serve as potent reminders of your goals and aspirations. When you repeat these affirmations daily, you also reinforce a proactive mindset, allowing you to embrace the challenges of the detox phase as opportunities for personal development rather than mere obstacles to overcome. While you can create your own inspiring phrases, here is a list of possible affirmations to enrich your morning routine:

- I am worthy of love, health, and happiness.
- With each passing day, I grow healthier and more resilient.

- I embrace change and trust the process of my transformation.

- I am capable of achieving my goals one step at a time.

- Today, I choose peace over stress and joy over fear and anxiety.

- I honor my body and mind by making choices that nourish me.

- I am surrounded by positivity and support as I embark on my alcohol-free journey.

- I have the power to create the life I desire, free from addiction.

- Each challenge I face is an opportunity to learn and grow.

- I am in control of my thoughts and reactions; I choose empowerment.

Incorporating affirmations into your morning routine can help solidify a constructive mindset, inspire motivation, and foster a profound sense of agency as you navigate the detox process and beyond.

Gratitude as a Resource

In addition to incorporating positive affirmations into your routine, gratitude practices can also help redirect your focus from daily struggles to moments of progress and small victories. Writing down things you're grateful for each day allows you to celebrate even the tiniest steps forward, as well as focus on resources rather than lack, fostering a sense of accomplishment and positivity. By concentrating on gratitude, you shift your perspective from what you have not yet accomplished to recognizing the abundance and strength already present in your life. Over time, this practice strengthens your ability to find joy in simple experiences, which is often essential when overcoming addictive behaviors.

One way to incorporate gratitude into your routine is through writing or logging what you're grateful for at the same time daily. Consider dedicating a portion of your journal to specific examples that highlight gratitude and personal growth. For instance, you might jot down three things you're thankful for each day, from supportive relationships to personal achievements, such as choosing a healthy meal or completing a workout. You can also reflect on any positive interactions, acts of kindness, or moments of resilience—

perhaps noting how you handled a challenging situation without turning to alcohol. Additionally, a gratitude log could include goals for the day or affirmations of self-love and encouragement, creating a comprehensive picture of your emotional landscape. Over time, this practice strengthens your ability to find joy in simple every day.

Visualization Techniques

Visualization practices can further enhance your commitment to sobriety by helping you imagine the successful outcome of your recovery journey. Picture yourself enjoying healthy relationships, excelling at work, and embracing a life filled with purpose and fulfillment—attributes that become more achievable through sobriety. Visualization isn't just about dreaming but involves vividly imagining the tangible benefits and changes that come with sustaining recovery to shift your expectations and actions. For instance, if you envision yourself waking up refreshed, engaging effortlessly in social situations without relying on alcohol, or conquering personal and professional milestones, it becomes easier to do so in actual life. These images also become motivators that drive you to persist, even when faced with temptation or doubt.

Daily Emotional Check-Ins

Establishing daily check-ins offers yet another layer of support in building self-awareness and promoting personal growth. By setting aside time, either each morning or evening to assess your thoughts and feelings, you gain insight into your emotional triggers and patterns, allowing for more informed decision-making and adaptive coping strategies. Reflective questions such as "What emotions did I experience today?" or "How did I handle challenging situations?" guide you in understanding your inner world more deeply, ultimately contributing to enhanced emotional intelligence and stability.

These mindset practices all equip you with tools to overcome hurdles with grace and determination. The benefits, while immediate, extend beyond the initial detox phase, providing long-lasting resilience against future challenges related to sobriety. By adopting these exercises into your daily routine, you empower yourself to embrace long-term change wholeheartedly.

The First Steps of a Winding Path

As you embark on this journey, remember that progress is not always linear. There will be days of triumph and, inevitably, days of struggle. However, armed with knowledge of common challenges and an intentional mindset, you're better prepared to face what comes your way and maintain the strength necessary for sustained recovery.

Navigating through the initial week of detox can feel like climbing a steep mountain, but it's during this time that you uncover true strength and transformation. From headaches and fatigue to mood swings and anxiety, these symptoms are temporary challenges on your path to healing. Embracing them as part of your journey can transform moments of discomfort into stepping stones towards recovery.

By focusing on day-to-day in these early moments of your alcohol-free life, you set a solid foundation for sustainable sobriety. The first week may be daunting, but its rewards are profound, laying the groundwork for a healthier, alcohol-free life. Celebrate every small victory and keep envisioning the brighter future ahead—you're taking courageous steps toward improving your life.

Chapter 5:
Replacing the Ritual—What to Do Instead of Drinking

It's Friday evening, and a long workweek has finally wound down. As you walk into the kitchen, you instinctively reach for a glass—out of habit, not hunger, or thirst, but simply because it's what you always do. For many, this moment feels automatic, a ritual etched so deeply into your routine that it's hard to imagine it any other way. But what if that instinct, the moment right before what used to be the pour, could become something else entirely?

Creating new habits that don't rely on alcohol can often be best achieved by finding replacements for the ritual of drinking. As we've discovered in the previous chapter, not only are these patterns deeply ingrained, but our neurochemistry has helped turn them into automatic responses to various triggers. s. Breaking away from these habits requires recognizing them for what they are and, through understanding that they don't serve a beneficial function in our lives, gently replacing them with habits that do. By viewing drinking as something we can choose to change rather than an unavoidable part of life, we support the process of transformation through both introspection and action. While alcohol has, up until this point, become embedded into our rituals and routines, we are rewriting those moments in ways that better serve our well-being.

Identifying Your Alcohol Rituals

Recognizing the habitual nature of drinking is a fundamental step in understanding and ultimately changing one's relationship with alcohol. Many individuals find themselves reaching for a drink in response to specific triggers rather than an actual necessity. This can often start as a seemingly harmless pattern, but evolve into a deeply ingrained habit that feels hard to break. It's critical to acknowledge that these triggers are often embedded in daily life, waiting quietly in moments of stress, gatherings with friends, or even during certain times of the day when the body and mind have been conditioned to expect alcohol.

Drinking cues can be internal or external. Internal cues often involve emotions such as anxiety, boredom, loneliness, or even celebration—feelings that might seem to call for a drink as a coping mechanism or reward. External prompts to drink, on the other hand, include social cues, environmental factors, or specific routines. For example, seeing others drink at a party, hearing the clink of ice in a glass, or simply unwinding after work at the same spot where you often enjoy a drink can activate these patterns.

To begin dismantling these habits, it's helpful to keep a log of when and why you reach for alcohol. Note the time, location, emotional state, and context. Are you pouring a drink to escape stress, to feel more confident in social settings, or because the act itself feels comforting and familiar? Identifying patterns in your triggers can illuminate the moments when alcohol serves as more than a beverage—it becomes a response to unmet needs or unresolved emotions.

Understanding your rituals surrounding alcohol is equally important. A ritual is not just the act of drinking but the entire sequence of behaviors surrounding it. Perhaps it's the ceremony of selecting a glass, the motion of opening a bottle, or the way you pair alcohol with certain activities like watching TV or preparing dinner. These rituals can hold emotional significance, making them feel comforting or even sacred. Acknowledging these associations allows you to see how they may reinforce your habits and offers an opportunity to reframe them.

The next step is to challenge these triggers and rituals by questioning their purpose. Ask yourself—does drinking truly address the need behind the trigger, or is it a temporary solution that creates more challenges in the long run? Recognizing this distinction helps you take control of your choices, opening the door to healthier alternatives that better serve your well-being. With this awareness, the path toward change becomes clearer. By identifying and understanding your unique triggers and rituals, you can begin to dismantle their hold and replace them with new, supportive habits that empower you to create the life you truly want.

Trigger Awareness

In addition to having rituals and routines that revolve around alcohol, each person typically has unexpected moments that can also trigger an urge to drink. While we'll explore these triggers in more depth in the next chapter, it's important to take a look at how they inform our routines and rituals. Stress is a common culprit. After a long day at work or dealing with personal challenges, a glass of wine or a beer might seem like an easy way to unwind and often becomes an evening ritual. However, it's important to understand that using alcohol as a stress reliever can become a crutch, masking problems rather than addressing them. By recognizing stress as a trigger, individuals can begin to explore healthier coping mechanisms. Breathing exercises, a short walk, or simply talking to a friend can be just as effective in easing tension without the negative consequences associated with drinking.

Social situations also play a significant role. These environments often encourage drinking, whether through peer pressure, tradition, or simply habit. Understanding this can empower you to navigate such scenarios with greater awareness. If you're someone who associates social gatherings with drinking, it might be helpful to prepare ahead of time. Bring your own non-alcoholic beverage, suggest meeting in a place where drinking isn't the main activity, or practice polite ways to decline a drink. Through this, you'll be fostering a sense of control over your actions and reducing the chance of giving in to habitual drinking.

Understanding these additional prompts to drink not only aids in managing and reducing cravings effectively but also heightens overall self-awareness in a way that can be of benefit on the longer journey of sobriety. When you recognize a trigger, you can pause, reflect, and make a conscious decision about how to respond. Instead of reacting automatically by reaching for a drink, you grant yourself the opportunity to choose differently. This shift from automaticity to intentionality is crucial in regaining control over drinking habits.

Realizing that you have the ability to identify and counteract triggers brings a renewed sense of agency and can be deeply empowering. It allows you to take back control, set clearer boundaries, and move with more intention towards a sober life that aligns with your values and aspirations. The journey only begins with identifying what prompts your desire to drink.

Once you have identified these additional situational triggers, you can proactively plan and respond to them—a key strategy for maintaining sobriety. For example, if social events are a challenge, consider bringing along a supportive friend who understands your goals and can help keep you accountable. If stress is your primary trigger, prepare a list of go-to alternate activities to provide relief and relaxation. Having this plan in place makes it easier to stay committed to your intentions when faced with temptation.

Rituals to Replace Drinking

Forming new routines to replace old habits associated with alcohol is a crucial step in maintaining a healthy and sober lifestyle, but after years of drinking, it can sometimes be challenging to envision doing anything else. This section will provide suggestions for replacements, as well as details on how they can be implemented in a way that is most likely to be both practical and effective.

Because drinking involves a ritual of consuming a beverage, one of the most effective replacement rituals early on can be to choose a soothing, healthy beverage for moments when you used to imbibe. For instance, many individuals find comfort and satisfaction in replacing their evening drink with a calming ritual, like brewing a warm cup of herbal tea. Or, if you typically enjoy a bubbly beverage, consider replacing alcohol with a fizzy fruit-flavored kombucha that supports your gut health. This simple act not only replaces alcohol but also creates a moment of mindfulness—focusing on the aroma, the warmth, and the process can be incredibly soothing. Additionally, both tea and kombucha have beneficial health impacts, making this replacement even more useful.

If alcohol rituals occur during stressful moments, exercise can be a great substitute. Physical activity is not only a powerful tool for those looking to fill the time once spent drinking, and it often releases endorphins that have a stress relief effect. Whether it's a brisk run, a hike through the park, a yoga class, or lifting weights at the gym, exercise is a natural mood lifter that can fill the space when you'd have picked up a drink in the past. Not only does this improve physical health, but it also helps reduce your baseline stress and anxiety. Moreover, setting personal fitness goals provides a sense of achievement and measurable progression that can help maintain motivation.

Reading is another excellent alternative. Fiction novels can offer an escape into different worlds while stimulating the mind. Picking up a good book during evenings or weekends when one might typically drink can become a treasured ritual, replacing the association of relaxation with alcohol. Immersing yourself in fiction can provide solace, inspiration, or simply a way to unwind, while nonfiction allows you to explore new ideas and perspectives.

For those looking to expand their horizons, diving into non-fiction resources about a new topic or reading about an unfamiliar area of expertise can be particularly rewarding. Whether learning a new language, researching the details of a historical event of interest, or mastering practical skills like cooking, gardening, or financial planning, this type of focused learning offers both mental stimulation and personal growth. This practice not only shifts your focus away from drinking, but also builds a sense of accomplishment and curiosity that enriches your life as a whole.

Mindfulness practices like meditation can be great practices for those seeking emotional balance and stress relief and can serve as substitute ways to unwind at the end of the day. Various techniques such as guided meditation, deep breathing exercises, or even mindful walking can help individuals center themselves, reducing the impulse to turn to alcohol as a quick fix for emotional distress. Starting with just a few minutes each day and gradually increasing the duration can make these practices a staple in daily life, offering serenity and clarity.

Social Substitutes

Social interaction is another domain where alcohol often plays a key role and can be challenging to replace. To mitigate dependency, exploring alcohol-free events in the early stages of your sobriety can be useful. Many health-conscious communities offer gatherings, such as movie nights, game nights, or craft workshops, specifically designed to be enjoyable without alcohol consumption. These events provide genuine connections based on mutual interests and shared experiences rather than drinks. Additionally, if these events are limited in your area, you can consider organizing such events yourself to encourage others to participate in a healthier lifestyle, strengthening social bonds in novel ways.

Seek out local community boards or online platforms to discover upcoming alcohol-free events. Consider joining clubs or groups that align with personal interests or new skills you'd like to learn, which can also be a gateway to forming lasting connections. As you develop new skills, set achievable goals and track progress to keep motivation high. Celebrate milestones reached along the way, however small they may seem. This positive reinforcement strengthens commitment and highlights how far you've come since deciding to pursue a life without alcohol.

Honoring Your Commitment to New Habits

Building a life that supports sobriety involves more than just removing alcohol from the equation; it requires laying down new, positive activities to take its place, and it also requires sticking to those activities long enough for them to become habits. This transformation can be achieved by applying habit formation principles. Understanding the mechanics of habit formation can aid individuals in more deliberately crafting daily routines that promote health and wellness, steering away from the automatic pull towards alcohol. Over time, these new actions can become second nature, replacing the urge to drink with the inclination to engage in activities that reinforce your commitment to sobriety.

Setting clear goals can be a great foundation, providing motivation and direction for those transitioning into a lifestyle free from alcohol. It's important to begin by defining what you want to achieve in clear, manageable terms. Whether it's committing to a certain number of days of a certain activity or aiming to achieve certain physical health goals through your exercise routine, setting realistic and measurable goals helps maintain focus and momentum and can shift your energy to what you want to achieve rather than what you'd like to avoid.

Writing these goals down can create a tangible reminder of your intentions, helping to keep motivation high even when challenges arise. It can also be helpful to break down goals and habit development into increments that allow you to track your progress. For example, someone might set a goal to attend an exercise class three times a week. With each session completed, the sense of accomplishment grows, reinforcing the decision to prioritize personal well-being over previous habits. These smaller milestones are easier to track, making the journey toward a sober lifestyle feel less daunting and more achievable. As progress becomes visible, confidence builds, leading to increased resilience against the temptations of returning to old habits.

Accountability and Sustainability

In addition to establishing concrete and measurable goals, creating accountability systems with peers can significantly enhance one's commitment to achieving sobriety. Sharing your objectives and goals with others who understand the journey fosters a sense of community and support. This network might include friends, family members, or support groups committed to similar paths. Engaging with an accountability partner allows for mutual encouragement, sharing experiences, and celebrating successes together. Furthermore, having someone check in regularly can boost resolve during challenging moments, offering reminders of why these changes matter.

Whatever support you choose should be designed to fit your lifestyle and feel natural rather than forced. Some may find attending group meetings beneficial, where open discussions about struggles and victories provide shared learning experiences. Others may opt for a more confidential approach, like regular phone calls or text messages with a trusted friend who offers encouragement and constructive feedback. Having accountability systems in place that match your personality and preferences helps maintain perspective and motivation, ensuring that the journey toward sobriety remains a collaborative, supported effort rather than a solitary struggle.

Getting Stronger Day by Day

As we explored how drinking often becomes a habitual response to various routines, rituals, and common triggers rather than a conscious action, it's important to recognize that these habits can be powerful and deeply ingrained, identifying those moments when we feel compelled to drink can make change not only possible but highly beneficial to our overall wellness. By understanding our stressors, social pressures, and daily routines that tempt us toward alcohol, we gain control over our actions and increase our overall personal empowerment. This improved self-awareness allows us to make conscious decisions and follow through on them, reshaping how we navigate our entire lives. As we begin to shift from automatic responses to intentional choices, we not only reduce alcohol cravings but also strengthen our self-determination to live our lives by design.

Chapter 6: Week 2–Breaking Free From Triggers

———————◆◇◇◉◇◇◆———————

Alongside the ways in which alcohol can be embedded into our daily routines and rituals, some of the other moments that trigger us to crave alcohol can be more subtle. Learning to detect and break free from the myriad of external and internal triggers that lead us to drink can be a transformative journey, not just on the path to an alcohol-free life but also in our self-discovery and rediscovery while embracing a life of sobriety. Identifying what specifically drives us to reach for a drink may not always be straightforward or easy, but it is an essential step in reclaiming control over one's life.

In this chapter, the focus shifts to identifying and removing those triggers that subtly influence drinking habits, offering a detailed exploration of the various elements that contribute to this behavior. We'll also explore the complex interplay of various triggers—emotional highs and lows, social pressures, or even certain environments that effortlessly encourage the habit. By beginning to recognize and analyze these specific cues, we'll learn to disassemble and reinvent the patterns that have long guided our alcohol use, replacing these ingrained responses with healthier coping mechanisms.

Identifying Emotional Triggers

Understanding the specific cues that prompt drinking habits is essential for anyone on a recovery journey. Recognizing emotional triggers can be a significant step in realizing why one turns to alcohol. Often, emotions like stress, loneliness, or anxiety act as subconscious catalysts, nudging individuals toward drinking as a means of escape or relief (Sullivan et al., 2024). By more readily identifying these feelings, one begins to break down barriers, illuminating the reasons why alcohol has become a go-to solution. Begin by taking an inventory of moments that most lead to cravings. Perhaps after a tough day at work, stress levels peak, and the idea of unwinding with a drink feels automatic. Or, during moments of loneliness or boredom, reaching for a glass seems to fill a void.

Acknowledging these patterns with self-honesty can be a transformative act in itself, as it requires a willingness to look deeply into your own behaviors and confront uncomfortable truths. Self-honesty means stripping away justifications or excuses and instead facing the reality of how certain emotions or situations have been managed through alcohol. This level of introspection can be challenging, as it often uncovers vulnerabilities or unresolved issues that drinking may have masked. However, it is also profoundly empowering as you start to notice and correct your tendency to make excuses and become more determined.

When you are honest with yourself, you also gain clarity about the true motivations behind all of your habits, not just drinking. For example, you might realize that your evening glass of wine isn't just about unwinding—it's about avoiding the stress you feel from unresolved work pressures. Or that your tendency to drink at social events stems not from a love of the atmosphere but from discomfort with being fully present in a crowd. But, you also may notice that you make excuses to avoid uncomfortable situations in your life, such as pursuing goals that feel scary or giving up relationships that no longer serve you. The holistic awareness you gain as you face the feelings that trigger drinking with honesty can create a foundation for meaningful change, as it allows you to address the root causes of many of your undesired behaviors.

Identifying Social Triggers

In addition to emotional triggers, social dynamics often play a significant role in drinking habits. Identifying patterns of behavior in environments where alcohol is present can help prepare mentally for similar scenarios in the future. Social events, especially those involving family gatherings, parties, or even casual meet-ups with friends, often come with an unspoken expectation of drinking, and often, those around you have identified you as someone who drinks alongside them. This identity may be one you take on effortlessly, and shifting to accept a new role in social dynamics can create both internal resistance and pushback from those around you.

While potentially challenging, recognizing this enables individuals to prepare mentally before attending such occasions. One might reflect on past experiences, noting how peer pressure or the mere presence of alcohol influences their decisions. They may consider who is most likely to pressure them or ask unwelcome questions about their behavior. This awareness encourages proactive planning—perhaps opting for non-alcoholic drinks, rehearsing polite refusals, avoiding certain interactions that may feel pressured, and setting boundaries beforehand to maintain personal control throughout the event.

Identifying Environmental and Physical Triggers

Assessing environments that encourage drinking is another critical aspect. Places like bars or frequent parties naturally create settings where alcohol consumption feels normal or expected. People recovering from alcoholism might benefit from restructuring their social lives to minimize exposure to these high-risk environments. For instance, consider replacing a weekly bar night with a movie night or a shared meal at a friend's home.

Physical triggers—those tied to specific settings, objects, or sensory experiences—can be just as powerful as social triggers in prompting the urge to drink. These triggers often develop through repetition, with certain physical elements becoming strongly associated with the act of drinking (Merrill et al. 2013). Identifying and addressing these cues is a critical step in breaking the cycle of habitual alcohol consumption. For instance, certain locations in your home may become linked to drinking routines. A favorite chair where you always sipped wine after a long day or a particular corner of the kitchen where you kept the liquor bottles can evoke cravings simply by being in those spaces.

Rearranging furniture or repurposing these areas can help break the mental connection. Turning the chair into a spot for reading or adding fresh decor to the kitchen can give these spaces a new, positive identity.

Even objects can serve as potent physical triggers. Glassware like wine glasses, cocktail shakers, or even a specific bottle opener may prompt memories and associations with drinking. Replacing these items with alternatives—such as new mugs for tea or water bottles—creates a fresh start and minimizes exposure to reminders of past habits. For example, having a selection of fun or elegant non-alcoholic drinkware can make a significant psychological difference.

Sensory experiences, such as the taste or smell of alcohol, are another common physical trigger. The scent of a particular whiskey or the flavor of a favorite beer might bring on cravings. Paying attention to lighting and ambiance can also make a difference. Dim lighting, candles, or even certain playlists might evoke memories of drinking, creating a subtle but powerful urge. Experimenting with brighter lighting, uplifting music, or calming scents like lavender or eucalyptus can transform the mood and reduce triggers. Exploring non-alcoholic substitutes can help redirect these sensory associations. Mocktails with complex flavors or sparkling waters infused with herbs and fruit offer satisfying alternatives that engage the palate without feeding the urge to drink.

The time of day or weather can act as physical triggers. For example, a cold beer might feel inseparable from hot summer afternoons, while a glass of brandy might seem tied to cold winter evenings. Anticipating these moments and creating new rituals can prevent them from becoming stumbling blocks. A refreshing iced tea or a chilled soda can replace beer on a hot day, while a steaming cup of hot cocoa or spiced cider can fill the gap on a chilly night.

Mindful Awareness and Triggers

While the broad range of potential triggers can seem daunting, mindfulness practices and even journaling can be effective tools for increasing awareness of triggers and enhancing self-awareness to the point that triggers are easy to detect and sidestep. Because mindfulness practices like meditation or deep breathing involve paying attention to the present moment, we become more aware of our feelings and sensations, allowing us to witness our triggers without judgment.

By practicing mindfulness, individuals can learn to notice when cravings occur, what they are doing at the time, and how certain environments or interactions impact their desire to drink. Incorporating journaling or logging triggers alongside mindfulness practices allows for deeper reflection. Writing down thoughts and feelings provides clarity, helping to identify recurring themes or stressors linked to alcohol use. Over time, these practices strengthen self-awareness in real time, creating an automatic conscious response to triggering situations instead of reactive drinking behaviors.

Through this improved awareness, instead of turning to alcohol as an immediate fix, individuals can explore alternative methods of coping, such as creative outlets, exercise or support from friends and family. Behavioral patterns become clearer through this lens, allowing for targeted and personal solutions that support personal growth. By embracing mindfulness and journaling, the process of self-discovery isn't just about alcohol; and it becomes a process of opening up new paths for overall well-being.

Practical Tools for Managing Triggers

Breaking free from the triggers that lead to drinking is a significant step in the recovery journey. When you anticipate situations where alcohol might be present, visualizing and rehearsing these scenarios can be an effective way to alleviate anxiety before social events. Picture yourself confidently navigating through gatherings, refusing drinks with ease, and engaging in conversations without feeling the pressure to partake. This mental rehearsal helps build a sense of preparedness, allowing you to face real-life scenarios with greater resilience.

Rehearsal Methods

Visualizing social settings before they occur gives you a chance to think through various outcomes and plan your responses. Consider running through different scenarios in your mind: What will you say if you are offered a drink? How will you handle questions or curiosity about your choice not to drink? Rehearsing these responses not only builds confidence but also diminishes the fear of confrontation. When the real event unfolds, you'll find yourself better equipped to stand by your decision with clarity and calmness.

Incorporating techniques such as positive affirmations into your rehearsal process can further enhance your confidence. For instance, before attending an event, take a moment to breathe deeply and remind yourself of your strength and commitment to sobriety. You might say phrases like, "I am in control of my choices," or "I can enjoy myself without alcohol." Practicing these affirmations alongside your visualizations creates a powerful toolkit, reinforcing your resolve and making it easier to navigate challenging situations with a positive mindset. As you do so, imagine the scenario unfolding where you gracefully and easily abstain from alcohol during the event, setting the stage for something similarly effortless to occur in real life.

Mindfulness Methods

In conjunction with visualization, incorporating mindfulness techniques like deep breathing can prove crucial when you're confronted with triggers. Taking slow, deliberate breaths not only calms the mind but also helps you focus on the present moment, which can reduce the overwhelming urge to reach for a drink. Physical anchors, such as holding a stress ball or pressing your fingertips together, can also keep you grounded in the present moment. These small actions remind your body that it's okay to stay calm and composed, even in challenging environments.

Deep breathing serves as another powerful tool to employ in the moments when the urge to drink is strong. When faced with a trigger, consciously slowing your breath also reduces the feeling of anxiety and reactivity and helps diffuse the urgency of the situation. In essence, by focusing on your breath, you create a pause between feeling triggered and reacting impulsively. This simple act can transform moments of vulnerability and risk into opportunities for strength, grounding you in the present and reinforcing your commitment to making a new choice.

Social Support Systems and Exit Strategies

Pairing up with a sober buddy can offer both reassurance and support during challenging times. By having someone by your side who understands your struggles, you create a safety net, and an increased sense of accountability. These partnerships can also provide motivation, encouraging both parties to remain steadfast in their sobriety goals. It's beneficial to have this ally check in regularly, ensuring mutual encouragement and offering a listening ear when needed.

Another practical approach for addressing more challenging dynamics involves discussing pre-planned excuses and signal systems with supportive friends ahead of time. Specifically, before attending events where pressure to consume alcohol may be involved, you can decide on discreet signals or code words to alert each other when you need help exiting a triggering situation. Having these "escape plans" prepared ensures you don't feel trapped or obligated to stay in uncomfortable environments. Clear communication with trusted friends about your boundaries can also build more honesty and overall support in these relationships, offering them a chance to aid in your journey or even consider their own alcohol-free lifestyle.

Structure and awareness become useful when managing triggers, particularly when recognizing and addressing patterns of behavior that occur frequently. Acknowledging such behaviors enables you to prepare mentally and anticipate potential challenges. Additionally, identifying which friends are supportive versus those who enable drinking can influence your social choices significantly. Making informed decisions about whom you spend time with strengthens your resolve and enhances your ability to maintain sobriety.

In addition to discussing exit strategies with friends or supportive loved ones beforehand when entering potentially risky environments, it can be useful to pre-plan phrases or action steps you'll use if you need to cut conversations short or leave early.

This preparation empowers you with autonomy over your actions, ensuring you respect your boundaries without alienating others and are able to act swiftly, even in moments of pressure or discomfort.

Scripts and Strategies for Saying No

Refusing a drink can often feel daunting, especially for individuals on the path to recovery. But with pre-written responses at your disposal, you can reduce anxiety and navigate these situations more confidently. Let's start with simple phrases that pack a punch. A straightforward "No thanks, I'm good" or "I'm sticking to water tonight" can be surprisingly effective. These short, clear statements help minimize confrontation, allowing you to assert your decision without feeling the need to explain yourself. However, for various high-pressure situations or dynamics that are particularly challenging, having phrases prepared can be incredibly useful.

Practice Makes Perfect

Confidence is key in such interactions. Practicing key phrases beforehand can give you the assurance needed when faced with a direct offer of alcohol. If you have a high level of anxiety, consider role-playing scenarios with a friend or support group to get comfortable with these refusals. The more familiar you become with these phrases, the easier it will be to deliver them naturally in real-life situations.

However, there are times when a situation calls for more than just a quick refusal. In those moments, phrasing refusals empathetically can go a long way. Acknowledging others' choices while reinforcing your own boundaries demonstrates respect and understanding. For instance, saying something like, "I appreciate the offer, but I'm working on taking care of myself right now," allows you to set a boundary without passing judgment on others. Some examples of scripts that are assertive and assured include:

Short and Straightforward:

- "No, thank you."
- "I'm good with water, thanks!"
- "I don't drink."
- "I'll pass, but thanks for thinking of me."
- "Not tonight, I'm focusing on my health."

More Descriptive Responses:

- "I appreciate the offer, but I've decided to stay sober for my well-being."
- "Thanks, but I'm working on my fitness goals, and alcohol doesn't fit into that right now."
- "I really enjoy being present during events, and drinking doesn't help me do that."
- "I'm currently in recovery, so I'm choosing to avoid alcohol altogether. Thank you for understanding."
- "I love that you're enjoying yourself! I'm just taking a different path for my health at the moment."

Light-Hearted Scripts

Humor can be an ally in diffusing potential tension during such encounters. Incorporating light-heartedness into your refusals can turn what might be an awkward moment into a pleasant exchange. Jokingly saying something like, "No drinks for me—I'm saving my liver for science!" or "You know, someone has to drive everyone home!" can break the ice and promote levity. Humor not only makes the conversation lighter, but also showcases confidence and ease in your choice. Some potential responses that deploy humor to diffuse awkward alcohol moments include:

- "No, thanks—my dance moves are wild enough without any extra help!"
- "I'd love to join, but I have a strict 'no hangover' policy. It's been working wonders!"
- "I'm doing an experiment to see how much fun I can have without alcohol—so far, it's working!"
- "I promised my grandma I'd stay hydrated, and I take my promises seriously!"
- "Thanks for the offer, but I'm trying to break the world record for the longest sober time at an office party!"
- "I'll pass on the drink, but I'm all in for the dance-off later!"

Remember, each refusal, whether to the point or personal and transparent, strengthens your resolve and builds confidence in your ability to stay true to your goal of living without alcohol. With practice, facing these situations becomes less intimidating, empowering you to own your decisions proudly and potentially even inspiring others to consider the same. As you equip yourself with these strategies, you'll find that the anxiety surrounding drink refusals diminishes, replaced by a growing sense of self-assurance, resilience, and greater confidence.

Strength in Every Step

Throughout this chapter, we've delved deep into the intricacies of identifying and managing the triggers that often lead to drinking. Whether they're emotional cues like stress and loneliness or social situations where alcohol is readily available, recognizing these patterns is crucial on the path to recovery. By understanding what prompts your desire for alcohol, you open up new avenues for change. This awareness allows you to replace old habits with healthier alternatives, empowering you to live a more balanced life. In addition to understanding your triggers, the importance of preparation and support in managing them cannot be overstated. Visualizing scenarios and practicing refusal scripts equip you with confidence when faced with real-life situations. It's about building mental fortitude and having strategies ready so you're not caught off guard. Bringing in a trusted sober buddy or creating signal systems with friends adds another layer of support, reinforcing your commitment to sobriety. As you embrace these tools and insights, you're not only making informed decisions for yourself, but also setting an inspiring example for others on similar journeys.

Chapter 7:
Your Social Life—How to
Navigate a Boozy World

————— ✦◇◇◉◇◇✦ —————

Imagine walking into a party where laughter echoes through the air and glasses clink in celebration, yet you feel perfectly content with sparkling water in hand. In a world where alcohol often seems like the glue that holds social gatherings together, embracing sobriety can feel like swimming upstream. But what if the key wasn't avoiding these situations but redesigning your place within them?

Navigating a booze-filled world while maintaining your social life doesn't have to be a tightrope walk. For those committed to sobriety, the challenge lies not in saying no but in saying yes—to new ways of connecting, enjoying, and thriving without the influence of alcohol. The reality is that a vibrant, fulfilling social life is entirely possible without the buzz of a drink, and with the right mindset and strategies, you can shine in any setting without feeling out of place or pressured.

Preparing for Social Situations

Social gatherings can be a source of joy and connection, but for those maintaining an alcohol-free lifestyle, they can also pose challenges. With thoughtful preparation and a few key strategies, it's entirely possible to navigate these events while staying true to your goals. Entering a social setting where alcohol is present begins with mental preparation. Rehearsing responses to potential questions about your choice not to drink can significantly reduce anxiety and boost your confidence. For example, simple replies like, "I'm the designated driver tonight," or "I have an early morning tomorrow" are effective and easy to deliver. These responses not only provide a clear boundary but also steer the conversation in a neutral direction without inviting further discussion.

The environment you choose plays a significant role in your experience. When you have control over the location, aim for venues where alcohol isn't the primary focus, such as coffee shops, parks, or cultural spaces like museums and art galleries. These settings naturally encourage meaningful conversations and connections, keeping the spotlight on shared activities rather than drinks. For outings with friends, suggest alternatives like a hike, a group fitness class, or a movie night. These alcohol-free activities shift the focus to experiences, making it easier to enjoy the company without added pressure.

However, there will be times when you have little to no control over the setting, such as attending a wedding, work event, or party hosted by someone else. In these cases, preparation becomes even more critical. Before attending, familiarize yourself with the event's layout—whether there will be non-alcoholic drink options or spaces to step away if you feel overwhelmed. Arrive with a plan, such as identifying supportive people who know about your choice or having a trusted friend on standby to check in with. If you're unsure about the drink selection, consider bringing your own non-alcoholic beverage to ensure you have something you're comfortable with.

When navigating these less controllable environments, focus on what you can influence—your mindset, your responses, and your boundaries. Shifting attention to conversations, engaging with others, or participating in activities at the event can help create a fulfilling and positive experience despite the presence of alcohol.

Just as important as preparing for the event is planning a graceful way to leave if needed. Knowing you have an exit strategy in place provides peace of mind. It ensures you remain in control, especially if guests may start to become increasingly intoxicated and it causes you discomfort or to feel extra pressure. Whether it's letting the host know ahead of time that you'll need to leave early, arranging for a ride home, or simply having a polite excuse like needing to get some rest, having an anticipated departure plan can be a lifesaver. If the event becomes overwhelming, you'll feel empowered to leave on your terms, preserving your comfort and well-being.

The Importance of Taking Nothing Personally

When you decline alcohol, it's essential to remember that others' reactions may sometimes reflect their own sensitivities or internal struggles rather than being about you. For some, your choice to abstain might unintentionally highlight their own inability to fully manage their alcohol consumption or related insecurities, prompting defensive or even dismissive responses. Understanding this dynamic can help you avoid personalizing their reactions and maintain your focus on your journey.

For instance, a friend might joke or press you about your choice, not out of malice but because it challenges their perception of what's "normal" or expected in a social setting. They might even feel uncomfortable about their own relationship with alcohol and project that discomfort onto you. Recognizing this can help you approach these moments with empathy rather than frustration.

If someone reacts negatively or makes a comment, try to reframe the interaction in your mind—viewing it as their way of processing rather than a reflection of your worth or choices. Responses like, "I totally understand—it's just what works best for me right now," can affirm your decision without creating conflict.

It's also important to keep in mind that there are two sides to every coin and be sensitive to the fact that many individuals have felt pressure *not* to drink in the same way you might feel pressured *to* drink. If someone insists on offering you a drink or questions your decision, a gentle response like, "I'm just not drinking tonight, but I'm happy to enjoy the night with you," can ease the conversation without making anyone feel awkward or judged. This shows sensitivity to their potential discomfort while maintaining firm boundaries in your own choice.

Building mutual respect involves setting boundaries with grace. Gently remind others that everyone has their own path, and avoiding alcohol is part of yours. For example, you might say, "I really appreciate that you care enough to ask! This is just something I'm doing for myself, and it feels like the right decision for me." This not only reinforces your resolve but also opens the door for meaningful dialogue, creating an environment where personal choices are respected.

It's also helpful to have a sense of compassion when faced with challenging social dynamics. Acknowledge that you're navigating uncharted territory, where those closest to you may have a hard time accepting your new identity, and it's okay if others need time to adjust. By staying centered and not taking reactions personally, you model self-respect and give others space to reflect on their own perspectives.

Building Confidence and Setting Boundaries

Navigating a social world that often revolves around alcohol can feel like a blow to one's self-esteem, especially if you are used to being the life of the party and "fitting in." Being alcohol-free may require a new level of confidence in standing out and making choices that don't fit the norm. While this confidence will grow naturally over time, there are some strategies to support your self-esteem while you're getting used to your alcohol-free lifestyle.

Affirmative self-talk is a powerful tool to set the foundation for confidence in one's personal decisions. When an individual reminds themselves of their reasons for quitting alcohol—whether it's for health, family, or personal growth—it strengthens the resolve to stay sober (Sutton, 2018). Repeating positive affirmations like "I am strong," "I choose clarity over confusion," or "My choices reflect my values" can help internalize these commitments. This kind of self-encouragement fosters a mindset that sees sobriety as a positive and empowering choice rather than a limitation. Consider making the following statements to yourself when facing social challenges to your commitment to quit drinking:

- I am worthy of a healthy and fulfilling life.
- I embrace my choices and celebrate my journey.
- My strength lies in my ability to say no.
- I find joy in creating new experiences without alcohol.
- I am in control of my decisions and my future.

- I choose happiness and clarity every day.
- My commitment to sobriety enhances my relationships.
- I am proud of my progress and growth.
- Each day, I am becoming the best version of myself.
- I attract positive energy and relationships that support my sobriety.

Assertive Communication

Assertive communication is another fundamental skill in navigating a boozy environment. It involves using confident language and clear statements about one's choices concerning alcohol consumption. For example, saying "No, thank you, I don't drink" delivers a clear message without leaving room for negotiation. Practicing assertive communication helps convey respect for oneself and establishes boundaries with others. More importantly, it encourages individuals to stand firm in their decisions and reinforces the idea that their choices deserve respect.

Assertive communication contrasts with both aggressive and passive approaches, which can create tension or confusion. Aggressive communication, such as sharply saying, "I don't drink, and I don't understand why anyone else would," can alienate others and create unnecessary conflict. This approach may lead to defensive reactions, not only from those offering drinks, but also from people who may feel judged for their own choices. Additionally, communicating in a way that preemptively defends one's decision, such as stating, "I'm not drinking, and I don't owe you an explanation!" can have a similar effect and put others on edge unnecessarily.

On the other hand, passive communication, like avoiding the topic or saying, "I guess I'll just have water," may signal a lack of confidence in one's decision, leaving the door open for others to question or pressure further. While passive communication might seem easier in the short term, it undermines self-respect and doesn't fully establish the boundaries needed for healthy interactions in the future. Striking a balance with assertiveness—firmly stating your choice without belittling others or over-explaining—allows you to protect your decision while maintaining positive relationships.

Practicing healthy refusal techniques empowers individuals to decline alcohol offers confidently and without guilt. Simple but firm responses, such as "I'm not drinking tonight," are graceful yet decisive refusals. Practicing these refusals can make them feel more natural when the situation arises. Declining alcohol doesn't need to be confrontational or even challenging; instead, it can be an opportunity to calmly reaffirm personal commitments and communicate personal boundaries respectfully (**Rusbatch, 2024**).

The Power of Sober Friends

Beyond formal support groups, finding other sober people at social events can be a game-changer. It's often surprising how many individuals choose to forgo alcohol but may remain unnoticed in larger crowds. When you make a point to connect with sober individuals at events, you not only gain a sense of camaraderie but also create a safe space where your choice is validated. Sharing an alcohol-free drink and engaging in conversation with someone who understands the journey can help you feel more at ease and less isolated. Sometimes, these connections can be made even before the event by reaching out to friends or acquaintances who also value sobriety. When you do find them, it's a great opportunity to strengthen those connections, support one another, and reinforce your commitment to living alcohol-free. This shared experience can make navigating otherwise boozy events more enjoyable and help shift the focus from drinking to deeper, more meaningful connections.

Furthermore, having a list of alcohol-free venues to gather with friends can enhance the social experience without the presence of alcohol. Coffee shops, parks, or artistic venues often provide engaging environments where meaningful conversations can take place. By choosing settings that naturally de-emphasize alcohol, the focus shifts to connection and shared experiences rather than drinking. This strategy not only supports sobriety but also enriches social interactions through diversity and creativity.

Exploring Sober-Friendly Activities and Events

Navigating a social world often entwined with alcohol can be challenging, especially for those committed to sobriety. Nevertheless, one can still enjoy vibrant and fulfilling experiences without the influence of alcohol. Cultivating new hobbies and diversifying your interests is vital in this pursuit. Engaging in activities such as hiking allows you to connect with nature and improve your physical health. The calming effect of greenery can lower stress levels and provide a peaceful setting to bond with friends or family. Additionally, cooking classes or art workshops can ignite creativity and offer an exciting way to learn new skills. These activities do not only enrich your life, but also open up new avenues for socializing.

Another excellent way to maintain sobriety while enjoying social gatherings is by hosting sober events. Planning a game night where board games and card games take center stage can be incredibly entertaining and interactive. It shifts the focus from drinking to team play and creates a fun atmosphere that encourages laughter and connection. Likewise, organizing movie marathons can bring people together in the shared enjoyment of films. Choose themes that resonate with the group, set up cozy viewing areas, and perhaps include homemade snacks or themed potluck dishes. This approach fosters a sense of community and inclusion, demonstrating that gatherings don't have to revolve around alcohol to be enjoyable.

When planning these events, start by selecting a venue or environment conducive to fun without the reliance on alcohol. Choosing venues that naturally promote engagement in non-alcoholic activities ensures that all participants feel comfortable and excited about the event's purpose. Communication is also key; clearly convey the intention behind the gathering when inviting guests that alcohol not be included. This approach sets clear expectations and attracts attendees who appreciate and respect the environment you are aiming to create (Mosunic, 2024).

Potlucks can also be a delightful way to share meals and experiences. Encouraging attendees to bring their favorite dish engages everyone and introduces diverse flavors to the table. Sharing recipes and culinary creations sparks conversation and can lead to deeper connections, as cooking and eating together is inherently communal. Such gatherings prioritize interaction and enjoyment, ensuring everyone feels included regardless of their relationship with alcohol.

For those looking beyond personal gatherings, exploring local community events that are alcohol-free is another effective strategy. Many cities host festivals, concerts, and fairs where alcohol is either absent or not the main attraction. Attending these events supports a sober lifestyle while enjoying music, arts, and culture. Farmers' markets, outdoor theaters, and cultural exhibits are wonderful examples of gatherings where the emphasis is on experience and engagement rather than drinking. These outings can invigorate your social calendar, providing ample opportunities to meet new people who share similar interests or values (Mosunic, 2024).

Rising to the Occasion

In this chapter, we've explored how navigating social situations without alcohol can be not only manageable but also genuinely enjoyable. By preparing thoughtful responses to questions about your choice to abstain, you build the confidence to engage in conversations gracefully. Humor plays a key role in diffusing awkwardness and keeping interactions light-hearted and fun. Choosing venues that focus on activities, like art galleries or parks, enhances your experience, while simple tactics like carrying a non-alcoholic drink help you blend in seamlessly and minimize attention on your sobriety. An exit strategy ensures you can leave whenever necessary, prioritizing your comfort. Beyond these practical tips, building self-confidence, setting boundaries, and using assertive communication reinforce respect for your choices and strengthens your commitment to sobriety. Finding and connecting with sober allies offers valuable camaraderie and support, making social situations more enjoyable and less isolating. With a toolkit of healthy refusal techniques and alcohol-free settings, you can enjoy fulfilling, alcohol-free experiences that align with your authentic self and demonstrate that fun and meaningful connections are easily accessible without alcohol.

Chapter 8:
Week 3–the Physical and Mental Transformation

—————◆◇◇◉◇◇◆—————

While up until this point, we've discussed the challenges and hurdles of the first 30 days of giving up alcohol, around Week 3, you'll likely start to experience something wonderful—physical healing and renewal—as your body begins to function more optimally again. At this point in the journey, your body begins to regain its natural energy, shedding the fatigue and sluggishness that alcohol has caused. This revival includes not only your physical energy but also your emotional and mental energy. With each passing day, the fog lifts a little more, revealing a sharper focus and clarity of thought. Emotionally, by this point, you've likely experienced a shift towards equilibrium as irritability and reactivity wane, replaced by a sense of calm.

This chapter will explore the specifics of the physical, mental, and emotional transformations you'll experience around the third week after giving up alcohol and explore how these changes can be harnessed and maintained. Specifically, we'll take a look at how enhanced energy levels can lead to healthy engagement in physical activities and how improved mood can support and develop valuable relationships.

The Third-Week Shift

Around the third week after quitting drinking, most individuals will experience a turning point where the challenging detoxification process and cravings subside, and the body and mind begin to become invigorated. Around this time, many will experience a tangible boost in energy levels, which is markedly different from the fatigue and fog that can accompany the detox phase (Julius, 2024). This newfound vitality allows you to engage more actively in pursuits that were once hampered by lethargy.

This revitalization stems from several physiological changes occurring in the body. Alcohol disrupts energy metabolism by impairing mitochondrial function, the powerhouse of cells. Once alcohol is eliminated, these cellular structures can function more efficiently, leading to improved energy production. Additionally, the liver, a critical organ for detoxification, starts to repair itself after being overworked by processing alcohol. This allows it to more effectively regulate glucose levels and other metabolic processes, contributing to an overall sense of vitality (Sharp, 2024).

Simultaneously, the quality of sleep improves significantly. Alcohol, despite its sedative effects, disrupts the REM sleep cycle and impairs restorative sleep. By week three, the body often regains a more natural sleep rhythm, leading to deeper, more refreshing sleep. This, in turn, enhances mood and energy levels during waking hours.

With these changes, physical activity not only becomes feasible but can become more enjoyable than it has been in years, with many feeling a level of energy they haven't experienced since their youth. The body's improved oxygenation, reduced inflammation, and normalized stress hormone levels allow for greater endurance and mental clarity. Many who have spent years experiencing suboptimal functioning due to alcohol misuse find this newfound vitality both surprising and motivating, often realizing they had mistaken chronic lethargy for normalcy.

Emotionally, quitting alcohol brings about a much-needed balance by allowing the brain and body to restore equilibrium. One of the first noticeable changes is a reduction in irritability, a common symptom of alcohol consumption (Julius, 2024). Alcohol disrupts the production and regulation of key neurotransmitters, such as serotonin and dopamine, which are critical for mood stabilization. Over time, as these chemical imbalances are corrected, the brain begins to function more effectively, resulting in a more even-keeled emotional state (Koob, 2023). This recalibration enables you to respond to stress with greater composure and resilience.

Another profound benefit is the improvement in self-esteem, which often emerges as a byproduct of healthier lifestyle choices. Achieving physical milestones, such as clearer skin or increased energy, serves as visible proof of progress, providing a sense of accomplishment. Furthermore, abstaining from alcohol allows you to set and achieve personal goals, creating a positive feedback loop that enhances emotional stability (Wandler, 2024). As these changes take root, many experience a renewed sense of confidence and empowerment. This mental clarity makes it easier to face life's challenges head-on without resorting to alcohol as a coping mechanism. The ability to manage stressors effectively reinforces your resolve, helping to solidify your commitment to sobriety. In turn, this emotional transformation becomes a cornerstone of long-term self-improvement and personal growth, offering a sense of liberation and fulfillment.

Experiencing these many positive transformations can strengthen deepen your commitment to remaining sober. The physical manifestations of improved health serve as daily reminders of the benefits of an alcohol-free lifestyle, fostering a stronger appreciation for sobriety. Emotionally, your ability to maintain balance can make it easier to cope with many of the challenges that often trigger you to drink. Observing the direct link between giving up alcohol and the resulting enhancements in quality of life reinforces why the decision was made in the first place. This growing awareness not only solidifies personal resolve but also can inspire others around you who are likely to witness your newfound flourishing, potentially opening dialogues about why you chose to give up alcohol and how it's impacted you.

Specific Health Benefits After Quitting Alcohol

Experiencing a month of sobriety can bring profound changes to both your physical and mental well-being that are notable, such as improved energy and emotional calm. With alcohol no longer influencing your body, certain health markers see remarkable improvements. One significant area of enhancement is digestion. Alcohol often disrupts digestive function, leading to issues like bloating and discomfort. For instance, alcohol irritates the stomach lining, often causing gastritis or exacerbating acid reflux. Overconsumption can also impair the production of digestive enzymes by the pancreas, which are crucial for breaking down and absorbing nutrients from food. By abstaining from alcohol, you might notice a reduction in these symptoms as your stomach lining heals and inflammation decreases. Additionally, the restoration of enzyme production enhances the body's ability to digest and absorb essential nutrients, often leading to a boost in energy and overall vitality. Improvements in gut motility and microbiome balance further support smoother digestion, reducing bloating and other discomforts (Czepa, 2024).

Blood pressure also benefits enormously since the absence of alcohol allows your cardiovascular system to function more efficiently, reducing strain and promoting better heart health. Alcohol consumption is known to increase blood pressure over time, as it interferes with the balance of hormones responsible for regulating blood vessel constriction and relaxation. By removing alcohol from your system, blood vessels begin to relax, improving circulation and reducing overall strain on the heart (Begum, 2023).

Beyond blood pressure, sobriety also promotes improvements in other aspects of cardiovascular health. For instance, quitting alcohol can lower levels of triglycerides and bad cholesterol (LDL), both of which contribute to the buildup of plaque in arteries and increase the risk of heart disease. The inflammatory effects of alcohol on blood vessels and tissues are also mitigated, helping to reduce the risk of conditions such as atherosclerosis. Furthermore, improved heart function leads to better oxygen and nutrient delivery throughout the body, enhancing energy levels and overall vitality. These changes not only bolster long-term heart health but also provide immediate benefits, such as reduced fatigue and a greater capacity for physical activity.

Avoiding alcohol significantly reduces the risk of liver disease and liver cancer, two of the most serious health consequences of alcohol consumption. The ethanol in alcohol burdens the liver by creating toxic byproducts like acetaldehyde, which can cause inflammation, scarring, and cellular damage over time. Chronic alcohol use also interferes with the liver's ability to repair itself, increasing the risk of conditions like cirrhosis, which is a known precursor to liver cancer. By eliminating alcohol, the liver gets a much-needed opportunity to heal and regenerate. This recovery process allows it to resume its vital functions, including detoxifying the body and producing essential proteins with greater efficiency. Studies show that even a month of sobriety can lead to measurable improvements in liver health, such as decreased fat buildup and reduced inflammation (Sadick, 2024).

Weight and blood sugar regulation show significant improvements during sobriety. Alcohol is not only packed with empty calories but also disrupts metabolism, often leading to weight gain and fluctuations in blood sugar levels. By cutting out alcohol, you eliminate a major source of empty calorie intake, which can result in weight loss and increase your intake of nutritious calories at the same time. Additionally, alcohol impairs the liver's ability to regulate glucose, contributing to spikes and crashes in blood sugar. Removing alcohol allows your body to maintain steadier blood sugar levels, reducing cravings and improving overall metabolic health. Without the inhibition-lowering effects of alcohol, you're more likely to make healthier food choices, contributing to a balanced diet and further supporting weight and blood sugar management. These combined effects are often noticeable even after a short period of abstinence. For instance, 58% of participants in sobriety challenges reported weight loss as a benefit after just one month (Sadick, 2024).

Sobriety also quickly enhances the immune system, offering noticeable improvements in just a short time. Alcohol weakens the body's natural defenses by disrupting the production and function of immune cells, leaving you more vulnerable to infections. Once alcohol is eliminated, your immune system begins to recover rapidly, potentially leading to fewer colds and faster recovery from illnesses when they do occur. This swift rebuilding of immune strength is especially helpful during times of heightened health risks, such as flu season or global pandemics. By abstaining from alcohol, you can bolster your body's defenses, improving resilience against various diseases and promoting overall vitality and well-being (Wandler, 2024).

Self-Care Tips to Amplify the Benefits of Your Alcohol-Free Transformation

As you journey into the third week of recovery, it's essential to nurture both body and mind. This week marks a pivotal moment in your transformation. Your body and mind are beginning to heal, and actively participating in this healing process through actionable strategies can enhance your recovery journey significantly and amplify the benefits in a way that can be incredibly motivating and inspiring.

A good starting point is understanding the role of proper nutrition and hydration and finding ways to make maintaining both enjoyable. Nourishing your body with nutrient-dense foods is akin to fueling a machine with premium fuel; it optimizes functionality. For instance, antioxidant-rich foods like berries and leafy greens fight oxidative stress, while lean proteins such as chicken and fish aid repair and growth. Emphasize incorporating a variety of fruits, vegetables, lean proteins, and whole grains into your daily meals, focusing on preparing them lovingly and choosing options you genuinely enjoy. These foods provide essential vitamins and minerals necessary for detoxification and increased energy, and eating them can also represent your commitment to personal health.

Hydration, too, plays an integral role in flushing out toxins from your system. Drinking enough water not only helps maintain physiological balance but also improves mental clarity and mood stability. Aim for at least eight 8-ounce glasses of water daily, adjusting for personal needs and activity levels. To make staying hydrated more enjoyable, infuse your water with slices of fresh fruits like lemon, lime, or berries, or add a sprig of mint for a refreshing twist. You can also explore naturally flavored sparkling water or herbal teas to keep things interesting. Staying properly hydrated supports your body's natural detox processes, making you feel more energized and focused (Wandler, 2024).

In addition to basic physical self-care, consider treating yourself to relaxing rituals at this phase that reinforce your commitment to well-being. For example, consider creating a calming evening routine: light a scented candle, run a warm bath infused with Epsom salts and essential oils, sip on a hot tea, and play soothing music. These acts of care, while seemingly insignificant, can help signal to your body that you are committed to caring for it, reduce stress, and further improve sleep quality.

Lastly, treat this period as an opportunity to discover what truly soothes, nourishes, and energizes you. Experiment with different forms of self-care until you find the practices that resonate most deeply, and commit to integrating them into your lifestyle. These rituals not only amplify the benefits of your alcohol-free transformation, but also serve as daily reminders of the care you're dedicating to yourself through making the choice to live without alcohol.

Nurturing Transformation

As you move through week three, take a moment to reflect on the powerful changes already beginning to unfold and notice how you feel. Your body may feel more alive, no longer weighed down by alcohol's impacts, while your mind finds clearer, more balanced ground. With each day you choose to abstain from drinking, you're nurturing positive transformations—tangible boosts in health that make physical activities not just possible but pleasurable—and observing emotional shifts that help manage stress with newfound calm and composure. This period is more than just recovery; it's about rediscovery. You are beginning to unearth parts of yourself once obscured, embracing a lifestyle that supports both well-being and fulfillment. As you recognize these changes, the commitment to remain sober solidifies. Remember, every step forward strengthens your resilience and opens doors to a world unshadowed by alcohol, inviting joy and gratitude into your daily life.

Chapter 9:
Week 4–the Emotional Reset

——————————◆◇◇◉◇◇◆——————————

Regaining the ability to manage your emotions may be one of the most rewarding and beneficial aspects of moving beyond alcohol. In the past, alcohol may have served as a crutch, dulling both the peaks and troughs of the emotional experiences you faced each day. Free from its influence, there is an opportunity to reconnect with the full range of your authentic emotional experiences while also developing healthy strategies for coping and responding to each feeling as it arises. In this chapter, you will explore how breaking free from the numbing effects of alcohol enables a more genuine interaction with your emotions. By actively engaging with your feelings, you open pathways to healthier coping mechanisms that replace past habits of avoidance. This clearer connection to your authentic emotions will not only allow you to have a richer experience of life but will also support sound decision-making, aligning your choices with true values rather than impulses and reactions.

Emotional Clarity Post-Sobriety

At the core of your journey through a month of sobriety lies an unexpected and profoundly empowering gift: newfound emotional clarity. This clarity does not merely stem from the absence of alcohol but from the active engagement with your emotions, which previously may have been muted or distorted by drinking. Recognizing and identifying your emotions without alcohol serves as the foundation for connecting more deeply with your feelings and allows you to process them genuinely.

Opening to Deep Feelings

When we rely on alcohol as a means to cope, it often acts as a barrier, preventing us from feeling the full spectrum of our emotions. This can lead to emotional suppression or avoidance of dealing with challenging feelings, and in suppressing our challenging feelings, we also often mute our positive emotions at the same time. Without alcohol as a crutch, we are forced to release these barriers and regain an experience of emotions in their rawest form. While this can be daunting and quite uncomfortable initially, it opens the door to authentic understanding and deeper acceptance of your inner landscape.

By simply acknowledging these feelings, you grant yourself the space to learn what they are telling you about your needs and desires, fostering a deeper connection with yourself. This enhanced awareness of your emotions also supports healthier decision-making. When you're not influenced by alcohol, your mind becomes clearer and better equipped to evaluate situations objectively. You are able to see things as they are rather than through a haze of intoxication, which aids in making decisions that align with your true values and goals. Over time, this practice of mindful awareness and thoughtful decision-making can lead to significant personal growth and self-discovery. As you become more attuned to your emotions, you gain insights into patterns that have shaped your behavior, opening avenues for positive change and personal development.

Mindfully Expressing Emotions

Expressing emotions positively is another critical aspect of this process, playing a significant role in mental well-being by reducing frustration and anxiety. In sobriety, you cultivate the ability to express your emotions constructively, whether it's through talking to a trusted friend, engaging in creative outlets, or practicing reflective writing. This constructive expression helps prevent the build-up of suppressed emotions, which, if unaddressed, can manifest as anxiety, anger, or depression. Instead, you develop resilience, learning to navigate life's challenges with a balanced emotional response.

Mindfulness emerges as a powerful tool in enhancing this emotional awareness further. By promoting non-judgmental living in the moment, mindfulness encourages you to view your emotions as transient experiences rather than defining features. Engaging in mindfulness practices such as meditation or deep breathing allows you to observe your thoughts and feelings without immediate reaction or judgment. This creates a buffer between your emotions and your responses, providing a calm space where you can choose how to act rather than react impulsively.

In adopting mindfulness, you not only enhance your ability to understand your emotions but also foster a compassionate relationship with yourself. It teaches you to accept every feeling—be it joy, sadness, anger, or fear—as valid and part of the human experience. This acceptance is crucial in avoiding the pitfalls of harsh self-criticism or undue pressure. Instead of seeing emotions as obstacles, they become valuable teachers, guiding you toward greater self-awareness and confidence in handling whatever life presents.

Combining emotional clarity with mindfulness, you create a dynamic framework for personal well-being during this sober journey. This synergy supports a stable emotional foundation, enabling you to face daily challenges with strength and adaptability. Furthermore, it positions you to recognize moments when old habits might resurface, equipping you with strategies to redirect those tendencies positively.

As you continue to explore this path, remember that every step forward, no matter how small, contributes to your newfound understanding and empowerment. This journey is uniquely yours, one that brings immeasurable growth and fulfillment beyond the shadow of alcohol. Through the lens of clarity, you find new opportunities to connect, grow, and thrive in ways that elevate your entire being, reflecting the profound potential within a life freed from the grasp of alcohol-induced dullness.

Coping With Stress and Depression

Navigating life without relying on alcohol can be challenging, especially when dealing with stress and depression. Understanding how to manage these emotions constructively is key to a successful recovery journey. By identifying stress triggers, you empower yourself to develop effective coping strategies that prevent overwhelming situations from taking control. Reflect on your daily activities: are there specific scenarios or interactions that consistently cause tension? Once identified, you can proactively address or avoid them altogether.

Physical activity plays a critical role in managing stress naturally. Engaging in exercise not only elevates your mood by releasing endorphins but also offers a healthy outlet to channel frustrations. You don't need a rigorous workout regimen—even a leisurely walk can help reduce stress. Alongside physical activity, creative outlets such as painting, writing, or playing music can provide equally powerful emotional benefits. These activities offer a chance to escape, relax, and find joy beyond the confines of daily pressures.

Another important aspect of stress management is diet. A balanced diet helps maintain energy levels and improves mood stability. When stressed, it's tempting to reach for comfort foods high in fats and sugars, but these can make you feel sluggish over time. Instead, focus on nourishing your body with whole foods, including plenty of fruits, vegetables, and proteins, which provide essential nutrients that support mental health.

The Power of Routine and Structure

Building and maintaining a daily routine can add structure to your life, balancing your responsibilities with self-care. This balance helps create a sense of normalcy, reducing feelings of chaos and unpredictability that might lead you back to old habits. Consider scheduling regular mindfulness practices, known for enhancing stress management skills. Mindfulness involves focusing on the present moment without judgment—it encourages you to breathe, observe, and let go of tension.

Getting adequate sleep is also essential for emotional well-being. Sleep deprivation can exacerbate stress levels, so prioritize getting quality rest. Establishing a relaxing bedtime routine without electronics can improve sleep quality, helping you start each day refreshed and more equipped to handle stress.

Open to Receiving Support

Maintaining a supportive network is another important step in overcoming dependency on alcohol for emotional regulation and one that can often be more readily established when we tune back into our emotions and connect more genuinely with our true feelings. Friends, family, and support groups offer encouragement and hold you accountable. Friends, family, and support groups can offer encouragement and hold you accountable, providing a foundation of trust and understanding as you navigate the challenges of an alcohol-free life. These relationships remind you that you are not alone, supporting a sense of belonging and reassurance during difficult moments.

In addition to personal connections, professional help can be invaluable, particularly when overwhelming emotions arise during your transition. Trained therapists specializing in addiction or recovery are equipped to guide you through the process of rebuilding your emotional resilience and addressing complex feelings that surface. Alcohol is often used to suppress trauma or mental health struggles, which may be better addressed with the help of specialized care. Professional support can provide targeted strategies for managing depression and other challenges, empowering you to confront these issues directly. Remember, reaching out for help is an act of courage and strength—it's an essential step toward reclaiming your emotional well-being.

The Journey Is Personal

Creating a personalized toolbox of strategies can provide immediate resources during challenging moments, ensuring you have the support needed to stay on track. Creative hobbies not only serve as an excellent stress reliever, but also promote self-exploration and personal growth. Finding enjoyment in activities like gardening, drawing, or crafting can distract from daily stresses and fill your home with positivity. Hobbies that engage both the mind and body are particularly beneficial, allowing for simultaneous relaxation and stimulation.

Combining these methods equips you with a comprehensive set of tools to manage stress and depression effectively, allowing natural processes to take precedence over past reliance on alcohol. As you progress through your recovery, it's important to celebrate small victories and acknowledge progress, no matter how minor they may seem. Recognizing achievements strengthens resilience and builds confidence, reinforcing the belief that living without alcohol is not just possible, but fulfilling.

Additional Practices to Support Emotional Health

In this phase of emotional reset, it's important to focus on empowering yourself with exercises designed to build resilience in your daily life. One such method is gratitude journaling. This practice can significantly impact your outlook by shifting your focus from negative thoughts to positive aspects of your life. By regularly jotting down things you are grateful for, whether it's a sunny morning or a supportive friend, you train your mind to see the brighter side of any situation. This simple shift can gradually enhance your overall mood and increase happiness by reducing stress and promoting a sense of well-being.

Another powerful tool in building emotional resilience is the implementation of Cognitive Behavioral Techniques (CBT). These methods play a critical role in altering negative thought patterns that may have been ingrained over years of reliance on alcohol. CBT encourages introspection and helps you challenge unhelpful automatic thoughts, offering a pathway to transform them into more constructive responses. For instance, the process of cognitive restructuring allows you to question and replace harmful beliefs with balanced thoughts, leading to improved emotional responses (Merrill & Thomas, 2013). By practicing these techniques, you establish a healthier dialogue within yourself, which leads to better emotional management and more rational reactions in various situations.

Consider starting with thought records, where you document a recurring negative belief alongside evidence supporting and contradicting it. This exercise compels you to critically evaluate the legitimacy of each thought, nudging you towards balanced conclusions. Moreover, behavioral experiments allow you to test different thinking approaches, comparing their outcomes to discern which path yields constructive results. As you refine these abilities, emotional setbacks lose their grip, replaced by logic-driven analysis and adaptive thinking (Volkow et al., 2019).

Visualization techniques also offer an effective strategy for fortifying emotional resilience. By visualizing yourself handling challenging scenarios calmly and successfully, you cultivate a sense of preparedness and confidence. This mental rehearsal allows you to explore possible outcomes and rehearse your responses without any real-world consequences. Such visualization can create a calming effect, reducing anxiety when you face similar scenarios in reality. Over time, these mental exercises can become second nature, helping you manage stress and approach complexities with a composed mindset (Merrill & Thomas, 2013).

The use of visualization serves as a rehearsal for real-life encounters, setting mental groundwork that primes you for success. Devote time to vividly imagine challenging scenarios where your composure and decision-making shine. Visualize walking into a social gathering confidently, maintaining genuine conversations while expressing your emotions authentically. By doing so, you habituate your mind to these settings, reducing intimidation and anxiety when confronted with actual events. Envisioning mastery ensures that your emotional state remains steady amid uncertainties, fostering growth in resilience and self-assurance.

Incorporating gratitude journaling into your routine can also support a positive perspective shift. Spend a few moments each day reflecting on what brings you joy or comfort. This act of acknowledgment isn't just about listing favorable events but delving into the emotions they evoke. How did it make you feel? What made this moment special? By exploring these questions, you reinforce positive neural pathways, diminishing the weight carried by negativity. As days pass, you'll notice an amplified appreciation for life, encouraging an optimistic viewpoint that naturally influences behavior and choices toward sobriety (Fisher, 2023).

The process of recovering our emotional wellness is often not straightforward, and it can help to think of each of these strategies as tools that we can experiment with and apply as they offer readily accessible resources during challenging times. Think of this toolbox as an array of coping mechanisms personalized to suit your emotional needs and strengths. Whether it's taking deep breaths, recalling a successful past encounter, or engaging in a brief meditation session, having diverse tools at your disposal enables you to address emotional difficulties promptly and efficiently. This proactive approach ensures you are not left searching for solutions amidst turmoil, but rather equipped to handle emotions with foresight and understanding.

Essentially, constructing a tailored emotional toolkit involves recognizing which strategies resonate most strongly with you and your unique needs. Each person's journey in emotional recovery is different, demanding individualized support systems. Evaluate an assortment of techniques—mindfulness, breathing exercises, reframing thoughts—and identify those that best align with your personality and lifestyle. Test them individually, then in combination, assess their impact on your mood and stress levels. This iterative process allows you to hone in on reliable measures that enhance your capacity to adapt and thrive without alcohol dependence.

As you integrate these practices, remember that consistency is key. Gradual yet persistent application nurtures lasting change, embedding new habits into your everyday interactions. Share your journey with trusted friends or support groups, providing mutual encouragement along the way. Celebrate milestones, no matter how small, and acknowledge challenges as stepping stones toward mastering emotional resilience. In doing so, you rebuild your life brick by brick, creating a foundation where sobriety is supported by mental strength and emotional clarity.

Showing Up Fully

As you move forward on the transformative journey of letting go of alcohol as a crutch and gaining emotional clarity, the process might feel intense at first, but it's integral to understanding your genuine needs and forming real and lasting connections that don't rely on drinking. Without the haze of intoxication, you're gifted with the ability to see situations clearly, leading to more informed decision-making that aligns with your true values and desires. By acknowledging this emotional landscape, you not only cultivate self-awareness, but also set the stage for personal growth and authentic living.

As the barriers that alcohol once maintained begin to crumble, you'll gain the opportunity to express your emotions in healthier ways—talking to friends, exploring creative outlets, or engaging with mindfulness practices. These new approaches empower you to handle life's challenges with resilience and composure. Remember that each emotion you uncover contributes to building a more conscious, fulfilling life. As you continue on this path, celebrate your progress, however small, knowing it enhances your understanding and confidence. Through this clarity, you open doors to connection, growth, and thriving beyond what alcohol once offered. Without alcohol, you make the space for your full self to show up, and as you learn to accept yourself, you are able to express and create in the world in a powerful new way.

Chapter 10:
The Financial Freedom Bonus

One potential benefit of quitting alcohol that is often overlooked is financial gain. Many people underestimate the impact that seemingly small expenses associated with drinking can have on their finances over time and how no longer drinking can even be a step towards financial freedom. Social outings, health care costs related to alcohol consumption, and even impaired productivity at work all contribute to limited finances. These hidden expenses accumulate gradually, often unnoticed, unless they become significant enough to impede one's financial goals.

This chapter delves into the nitty-gritty of these hidden costs, helping readers calculate their own "Sober Bonus"—the amount of money potentially saved when alcohol expenses are cut. It walks you through creating practical tools like monthly budgets and expense trackers, offering insights into how sobriety can transform personal finance. By exploring these aspects, individuals can gain clarity on how much money is truly devoted to maintaining a lifestyle that includes alcohol consumption.

Break Down the Hidden Costs of Drinking

When we think about financial freedom, we seldom consider the hidden costs entwined with alcohol consumption. To fully grasp the hidden financial impacts of drinking, one must look beyond the obvious price tags on bottle bar tabs the true cost of drinking lies in accumulated secondary expenses that silently drain savings over time.

To start with, many people underestimate how much they spend on social drinking (Blake, 2023). It's easy to lose track, as buying a couple of drinks weekly might seem insignificant at first. However, the expenses can quickly add up, especially when factoring in related costs. Socializing while drinking often involves more than just the cost of beverages. For example, meals or snacks purchased at bars or restaurants can significantly increase the bill. Additionally, there are often transportation expenses, such as taking a taxi, rideshare, or public transport home, particularly if drinking limits the ability to drive. Over time, these combined costs can amount to hundreds or even thousands of dollars annually, depending on frequency and habits.

These seemingly small expenditures can snowball into significant amounts over months or years. Imagine attending just one social event weekly and spending $50 each time on drinks and additional costs. That's $2,600 annually—a substantial sum that's often spent without a second thought. Two nights a week, and you've spent $5,200 extra in one year. Over a decade, without adjusting for increased prices or inflation, this habit alone could mean over $52,000 less in your account. For those looking toward financial stability and future planning, this significant sum of money could be earmarked for investments, debt repayment, or even an emergency fund.

Health issues that are worsened by alcohol consumption can also have a huge also play a significant role in one's financial state (Armstrong, 2024). As we've covered earlier, regular consumption increases the risk of numerous chronic health conditions, such as liver disease, heart problems, and certain types of cancer. Treating these illnesses typically involves ongoing medical expenses that can quickly deplete savings. The challenge isn't only the immediate expense but the potential long-term financial instability due to chronic health problems. Direct healthcare costs stemming from alcohol-attributable illnesses can also include hospitalization charges and lost wages, in addition to treatment costs, which are severely burdensome for any budget. For instance, dealing with heart disease might require frequent doctor appointments and daily medication, chipping away at once financial resources.

Subtle but Significant Professional Costs

Drinking affects more than health—it can take a costly toll on professional life. Absenteeism, hangovers, and diminished productivity impair job performance, potentially leading to lost wages or missed career advancements. These setbacks, though harder to quantify than social or health-related costs, can accumulate significantly (Armstrong, 2024).

Brain fog and reduced efficiency from drinking can create patterns of underperformance, eroding trust with colleagues and supervisors. Frequent lateness or absenteeism not only impacts earnings but also tarnishes professional reputations, limiting opportunities for promotions or raises. Over time, this loss of reliability may push valuable opportunities out of reach or even result in job loss, amplifying the financial consequences.

Calculate Your "Sober Bonus"

Now that we've established the many potential financial costs of drinking, imagine being able to redirect those funds towards meaningful goals or even investing in such a way that you are able to eventually achieve financial freedom. This concept can become more tangible by creating a monthly budget that intentionally omits alcohol-related expenses and quantifies the saved expenses. For individuals in recovery or those contemplating sobriety, this step marks the beginning of comprehensive financial wellness.

By monitoring and recording expenditures without alcohol, there's also an opportunity for clearer financial planning. One practical way to visualize these changes is by creating a monthly expense tracker dedicated to monitoring expenditures before and after sobriety. By systematically recording spending habits, individuals can gain clarity about where their money is going and reallocate funds to more meaningful purposes. Another powerful tool is conducting an analysis of previous vs. projected expenses. Many are shocked when they calculate how much they've been spending on alcohol over a year. Even a seemingly modest $50 per week translates to $2,600 annually—a sum that could significantly boost a savings account, reduce credit card debt or contribute to a home improvement project.

By redirecting funds previously used for alcohol, individuals often experience immediate financial relief while gaining greater control over their disposable income. For communities, collective savings can even open doors to group investments or initiatives that strengthen local networks and economic growth.

Quitting alcohol isn't just a personal choice—it's a financial strategy that redefines spending habits, fosters savings, and creates opportunities for growth. Whether through small wins like funding a family trip or significant milestones like building a retirement fund, the decision to quit drinking is an investment in a brighter and more secure future.

Reinvesting in Yourself

Financial freedom is not just about wealth; it's about making choices that enhance personal growth and emotional well-being. For those pursuing sobriety, redirecting money once spent on alcohol can lead to life-changing improvements. Here's how to invest those savings effectively.

Invest in health and wellness: Spending on gym memberships or personal training can boost energy, improve mood, and manage stress—key benefits for recovery. Exercise builds structure and discipline, aiding sobriety while enhancing overall well-being. Additionally, fitness-related expenses are often eligible for health reimbursement arrangements, reflecting their recognized importance.

Explore new hobbies: Engaging in creative pursuits like painting, cooking, or playing an instrument stimulates the mind and fosters a sense of accomplishment. Joining local classes or clubs can introduce you to like-minded individuals, supporting healthier, interest-driven social circles.

Build a supportive community: Redirect funds toward joining recovery groups or attending workshops that strengthen connections and accountability. These investments in your network provide emotional support and shared strategies for maintaining sobriety.

Improve financial literacy: Learning to budget, save, and invest equips you to make informed decisions. Financial workshops or online courses can empower you to navigate your finances confidently, ensuring your savings contribute to long-term goals.

Plan and save: Set a budget that prioritizes physical health, hobbies, and financial education while automating savings for future milestones like home ownership or retirement. By investing in yourself, you'll uncover new passions and strengths, transforming your life into one of resilience, fulfillment, and financial security.

Adding It All Up

Quitting alcohol not only liberates you from the grip of dependency but also unlocks surprising financial advantages. By consciously eliminating alcohol expenses, you're creating room for unexpected growth, fostering both immediate relief and future stability. The decision to go sober acts as a catalyst for financial wellness, providing a tangible boost to your wealth over time. Imagine redirecting your 'sober bonus' toward meaningful goals— whether it's building an emergency fund, paying off debt, or finally taking that dream vacation. These newfound savings serve as a stepping stone, supporting you in crafting a more secure, fulfilling lifestyle and a brighter, more prosperous tomorrow.

Chapter 11:
How to Handle Setbacks
–the Sober Mindset

————— ✦◇◇◉◇◇✦ —————

Handling setbacks is an essential aspect of the sober mindset, where slips are seen not as failures but as opportunities for growth and learning. This chapter dives into the journey of sobriety, emphasizing that stumbling doesn't mark the end of the path. It reassures readers that mistakes and setbacks are a natural part of the recovery process, which everyone can experience from time to time. By fostering a mindset that views these moments as valuable lessons rather than insurmountable obstacles, one can approach sobriety with a more forgiving and resilient attitude.

Developing a Sober Mindset

Embracing sobriety is like embarking on a lifelong journey fraught with challenges and triumphs. It's crucial to recognize that setbacks are part of this journey, not just obstacles, but opportunities for growth. When individuals encounter slips, it's tempting to see them as failures or reasons to give up. However, by understanding them as essential learning moments, one can pivot towards progress and resilience.

Slips may appear daunting, yet they offer a unique insight into the triggers and patterns that led to them. For instance, suppose someone finds themselves drinking after a stressful day at work. This isn't just a setback; it's an opportunity to identify stress as a trigger and explore healthier coping mechanisms. By reframing slip-ups this way, individuals are better equipped to navigate future challenges without succumbing to similar pitfalls. This recognition transforms what might feel like a defeat into a stepping stone toward a more robust and informed approach to sobriety.

Perfection is often mistakenly seen as the ultimate goal in recovery when, in reality, it's the pursuit of steady progress and a greater sense of presence that holds greater importance. Striving for perfection can lead to discouragement and a sense of failure when inevitable slip-ups occur. Instead, focusing on gradual improvement and awareness of each step of the journey allows for a more manageable path forward. Each small step, each decision made in favor of sobriety, contributes to building a healthier lifestyle over time.

Practicing mindfulness can be instrumental in this process. By staying present and attuned to thoughts and emotions, individuals gain a deeper understanding of their triggers and can intercept harmful thought patterns before they lead to action. Techniques like meditation and deep breathing help maintain emotional balance and composure, especially in difficult moments. Each mindful decision builds a healthier, more resilient lifestyle.

Forgiving oneself is a crucial step in the journey to sobriety. Letting go of guilt and shame reduces the emotional burden that can hinder progress. Embracing self-compassion allows individuals to release regret and focus on the future.

Self-forgiveness doesn't excuse past mistakes, but acknowledges imperfections as part of growth. By learning from these experiences, individuals strengthen their resolve and continue moving forward without being weighed down by past errors.

How to Effectively Handle Slip-Ups Without Shame

When setbacks occur, it is important to shift the focus from guilt and shame to actionable recovery. Developing a personalized action plan can significantly aid in navigating these challenging moments without succumbing to negative emotions. This plan should include an array of strategies that speak directly to your needs and circumstances. Begin by identifying the specific triggers or situations that led to the slip-up. Once these are recognized, you can brainstorm potential responses or alterations in behavior that could prevent similar occurrences in the future.

It's not uncommon to feel overwhelmed when things don't go as planned, but having a roadmap can offer reassurance and direction. Consider writing down your action plan step by step. For instance, if stress at work is a trigger, decide on practical ways to manage it, such as setting boundaries with colleagues or incorporating short mindfulness exercises into your day. By putting these strategies on paper, you create a commitment to yourself, which can be both empowering and soothing.

In addition to self-devised tactics, the importance of support systems plays as much of a role in overcoming setbacks as it does in the alcohol-free journey itself. Having trusted friends, family members, groups, or mentors to lean on can provide much-needed perspective and guidance. These individuals or networks can offer encouragement and remind you of your strengths and progress. Sometimes, simply talking about your experience with someone who understands can lift a significant weight off your shoulders.

Consider joining a supportive group where members share their journeys and strategies. Groups like Alcoholics Anonymous have long provided a platform for shared experiences and mutual support. If you're more comfortable with one-on-one interactions, finding a mentor who has navigated similar challenges can be especially beneficial. They can offer insights gained from their own experiences, providing practical advice and emotional support tailored to your journey.

Reflecting on personal goals after a setback is another essential strategy. It allows you to evaluate and adjust your objectives to align better with your current situation. This reflection isn't about criticizing past failures, but about understanding what shifts might be necessary to continue forward effectively. Ask yourself: What were my initial goals? How have they changed? What steps can I take to modify them in light of recent experiences? This process of reassessment empowers you to redefine success on your terms and may involve setting smaller, more measurable milestones to build confidence.

Practicing self-care post-slip is an integral component of recovering gracefully from setbacks. Often underestimated, exercise and nutrition play pivotal roles in maintaining mental and physical well-being. Jumping back into alcohol-free hobbies or activities that bring you joy and relaxation can complement these self-care practices and help to restabilize you after a slip-up. Whether it's painting, gardening, or listening to music, dedicating time to enjoyable pursuits can shift your attention back to recovery instead of the slip-up.

Give Yourself Grace

As we begin viewing slip-ups not as failures but as opportunities for growth, it becomes apparent that not only is sobriety a complex journey and that understanding setbacks can offer insights that can support us in the future. Personal triggers and coping mechanisms are key to progress. By shifting our perspective from seeking perfection to valuing steady improvement, we empower ourselves to respond with resilience rather than discouragement when obstacles arise. Practicing forgiveness and letting go of guilt allows us to focus on what's ahead, using past experiences to carve out a more successful journey. These strategies help frame setbacks as temporary detours rather than dead ends, reaffirming that slipping is not the end of the world but part of the winding journey to sobriety.

Chapter 12: Alcohol-Free for Life—the New You

———— ✦◇◇◉◇◇✦ ————

Embracing a sober lifestyle is about embarking on a profound journey of transformation. The decision to live alcohol-free goes beyond the simple act of abstaining; it is a commitment to reimagining and reshaping your life, fostering growth, and creating new pathways toward personal fulfillment. This transition represents an opportunity to rediscover your passions, realign your goals, and cultivate a life enriched with purpose and clarity. As you step onto this path, it's essential to recognize that each moment without alcohol is a celebration of your resilience and dedication to change. It's about embracing the new you—a version that thrives in the richness and abundance of a life unburdened by dependency.

Celebrate and Visualize Future Goals

Reflecting on your journey, including the challenges and victories, helps cultivate gratitude and reinforce personal growth. Keeping a journal can serve as a tangible reminder of your resilience and strength. Celebrating milestones—big or small—further solidifies your commitment. Organize a gathering with loved ones, indulge in a meaningful activity, or simply take a moment to honor your progress. These celebrations create cherished memories that enhance your sense of purpose.

Setting clear, attainable goals in health, relationships, and career can keep you motivated. Adopt healthier habits, strengthen bonds with loved ones, or pursue professional aspirations like further education or promotion. Achieving these goals boosts self-esteem and reinforces the rewards of sobriety. Visual reminders, like a vision board filled with inspiring images and quotes, can keep your goals front and center. Place it somewhere you'll see daily to maintain focus on your aspirations.

Sharing your story can inspire others and create a deeper sense of connection and community. Whether through a blog, support group, or conversation, opening up about your journey encourages others while affirming your growth. Surround yourself with supportive people who uplift you. Sobriety isn't just about absence—it's about an abundance of health, opportunity, and happiness. Celebrate your progress, cherish your victories, and step confidently into a thriving, alcohol-free life. Each step forward is a testament to your courage and determination.

Staying Motivated for Future Sobriety

Maintaining a commitment to an alcohol-free lifestyle is a powerful journey, rich with opportunities for personal growth and lasting change. Setting incremental, measurable goals is a powerful way to maintain momentum in your sobriety journey. Goals like learning a skill, pursuing education, or engaging in hobbies channel energy into productive outlets and build confidence. Whether training for a marathon or tackling smaller tasks align your objectives with your passions. These achievements, big or small, serve as lasting reminders of your ability to transform intentions into action, reinforcing self-belief and resilience.

Incorporating daily practices like affirmations and mindfulness can significantly enhance self-awareness and emotional regulation. Begin each day with positive affirmations, stating intentions such as "I am committed to my well-being" or "Today, I choose strength over temptation." These simple yet impactful statements can shift your mindset, setting a positive tone for the day ahead. Mindfulness practices, such as meditation or deep-breathing exercises, encourage presence and help you manage cravings and stress effectively.

Creating a reward system for sobriety milestones reinforces positive behavior and keeps motivation high. Set specific goals—like one week, one month, or six months sober—and celebrate each achievement with meaningful rewards, such as a new book, a small getaway, or a favorite activity with loved ones. These incentives turn the journey into manageable steps, boosting morale and providing tangible reminders of progress. Sharing these victories with your support network amplifies joy and strengthens your resolve through collective celebration.

Strong social connections are vital to your transformation. A supportive network provides encouragement and guidance during challenges. Join local or online support groups to share experiences and celebrate victories with those on a similar path. Open communication with family and friends about your needs and boundaries fosters their active involvement in your success. If your circle lacks understanding, professional counselors or therapists can offer valuable tools and support.

One Day at a Time

Quitting drinking rejuvenates the body, strengthens the mind, and frees the spirit. Physically, sobriety allows your body to heal, bringing renewed energy and improved overall health. Mentally, it sharpens your focus, restores clarity, and helps rebuild confidence in your abilities. Emotionally, it creates a space for authentic connections, inner peace, and a sense of purpose that may have felt out of reach.

These many changes, however, do not occur all at once, nor do they begin with grand gestures. Quitting drinking is a choice that occurs day by day. The first 30 days are your foundation, a period of self-discovery and resilience that will set the stage for each alcohol-free day to come. Each day in this first month is an opportunity to learn, grow, and prove to yourself that you are capable of thriving beyond the grip of addiction.

Remember, progress isn't about perfection; it's about perseverance and taking one step forward at a time. With each passing day, you build a life that is more rooted in health, authenticity, and joy—a life that reflects the best version of yourself. Sobriety isn't just the absence of alcohol; it's making more space in your life for everything that makes it truly meaningful.

Bonus I: Progress Tracker

This tracker is designed to help you monitor your progress, reflect on your journey, and celebrate the positive changes happening in your life during this 30-day alcohol-free challenge. Use it daily to record how you're feeling and note key achievements along the way.

How To Use the 30-Day Progress Tracker

- **Daily check-in:** Each day, fill in your mood, energy, sleep, cravings, and money saved.

- **Reflection**: Use the notes section to jot down thoughts, milestones, or gratitude.

- **Celebrate wins**: At the end of each week, reflect on your progress and acknowledge your successes.

Day	Mood (1-10)	Energy (1-10)	Sleep (Hours/quality)*	Cravings (None/moderate/strong)	Money saved ($)	Notes
Day 1						
Day 2						
Day 3						
Day 4						
Day 5						
Day 6						
Day 7						
Day 8						
Day 9						
Day 10						
Day 11						
Day 12						
Day 13						
Day 14						
Day 15						
Day 16						
Day 17						
Day 18						
Day 19						

Day 20					
Day 21					
Day 22					
Day 23					
Day 24					
Day 25					
Day 26					
Day 27					
Day 28					
Day 29					
Day 30					

Bonus II: Cravings Buster Tool

Cravings can be one of the toughest parts of staying alcohol-free, but they're also temporary. Use this quick-reference guide to handle cravings at the moment, shift your mindset, and stay on track with your 30-day challenge.

Mindset Shifts for Overcoming Cravings

1. Remember why you started

2. Reflect on your reasons for taking this challenge. How will you feel tomorrow if you stay strong today?

3. Cravings are not commands

4. A craving is a signal, not a necessity. It's your body adjusting, not demanding action.

5. This moment will pass

6. Cravings typically last 10–20 minutes. Focus on getting through this moment, knowing it's temporary.

Actionable Tips to Beat Cravings

1. Distract yourself

- Engage in an activity that occupies your hands and mind—knit, doodle, or play a game on your phone.

- Go for a brisk walk or do light exercise to shift your focus and release endorphins.

2. Hydrate

- Drink a large glass of water. Sometimes, cravings mask dehydration.

- Add lemon, cucumber, or mint for a refreshing twist.

3. Snack smart

- Reach for a healthy snack like almonds, fruit, or yogurt to curb hunger-related cravings.

- Choose something crunchy to keep your hands and mouth busy.

4. Deep breathing

- Practice the 4-7-8 method: inhale for 4 seconds, hold for 7, exhale for 8. Repeat three times.

- This calms your nervous system and shifts your focus inward.

5. "10-minute rule"

- Commit to waiting just 10 minutes before acting on the craving.

- Use the time to journal, meditate, or listen to a favorite song.

6. Call a support person

- Reach out to a friend, family member, or sponsor who supports your sobriety.

- Talking through your feelings can help dissolve the craving.

Emergency Questions for Mindset Recalibration

- "How will I feel tomorrow if I drink now?"

- "Is this worth undoing the progress I've made?"

- "What do I actually need right now—rest, connection, or distraction?"

Visualize Your Victory

Close your eyes and picture yourself at the end of the 30 days—healthier, happier, and empowered.

Cravings lose their grip when you focus on your ultimate goal.

Print or screenshot this tool so it's easily accessible when you need it most. With the right strategies, you can turn cravings into opportunities to reinforce your commitment to a better, alcohol-free life.

Bonus III: Sober Scripts

———————◆⬥◉⬥◆———————

Social situations can be challenging when you're navigating sobriety. Having a plan for how to say "no" to a drink makes it easier to handle these moments with confidence. Use these pre-written scripts to navigate common scenarios and build your social skills without compromising your commitment to staying alcohol-free.

At a Party

- **Polite and simple:**
- "No, thank you. I'm sticking to non-alcoholic drinks tonight."
- **Confident and firm:**
- "I'm on a health kick right now, so I'm skipping alcohol."
- **Redirect the focus:**
- "No, thanks! I'll grab a soda—what are you drinking?"

At a Work Event

- **Professional and neutral:**
- "I'm good with just water for now, but thank you!"
- **Health-oriented:**
- "I'm not drinking these days—trying to stay sharp for tomorrow."
- **Team player:**
- "I'm the designated driver tonight, so I'll stick to something non-alcoholic."

With Friends Who Know Your Drinking History

- **Honest and open:**
- "I've decided to take a break from drinking—it's been really good for me."
- **Lighthearted:**
- "I'm challenging myself to see how good life can be without alcohol. So far, so good!"
- **Supportive response:**
- "I appreciate your understanding—I'm really focused on my goals right now."

When Pressured by Someone Persistent

- **Direct and clear:**
- "I appreciate the offer, but I'm not drinking. Please respect that."
- **Humorous deflection:**
- "Thanks, but I'm not in the mood to regret anything tomorrow!"
- **Firm but polite:**
- "No, really, I'm fine. Let's not make this a big deal."

When Offered a Drink by Someone Unfamiliar With Your Sobriety

- **Nonchalant and brief:**
- "No, thanks—I'm good with what I have."
- **Social and casual:**
- "I don't drink, but I'd love a soda if you have one."
- **Honest but minimal:**
- "I'm alcohol-free these days—it's just a personal choice."

Quick Mindset Boosts for Social Situations

- "You don't owe anyone an explanation for your choices."

- "Saying 'no' shows strength, not weakness."

- "Your health and happiness are worth far more than a drink."

Rehearse these responses ahead of time so you feel prepared. Confidence grows when you're ready for the moment. You can even role-play with a trusted friend or practice in front of a mirror.

By using these scripts, you'll not only navigate social situations smoothly but also strengthen your commitment to living alcohol-free. You've got this!

Bonus IV:
Habit Replacement Worksheet

————— ◆◇◇◉◇◇◆ —————

Changing habits is a powerful step in your alcohol-free journey. Use this worksheet to identify the triggers, habits, and rewards associated with drinking and replace them with positive alternatives that align with your goals. By breaking old patterns and establishing new ones, you can create a healthier, more fulfilling lifestyle.

Step 1: Identify your habit loop

- **Trigger:** What prompts the habit? (e.g., stress, boredom, social pressure)
  Example: Feeling stressed after work.

- **Habit:** What action do you take in response to the trigger?
  Example: Pouring a glass of wine.

- **Reward:** What do you gain from the habit? (e.g., relaxation, distraction, social connection)
  Example: A sense of temporary relaxation.

Step 2: Reflect on the underlying need

- What are you truly seeking from this habit? *Example: I need a way to unwind and let go of stress.*

Step 3: Replace the habit

Choose a new, positive habit that satisfies the same need.

- **Trigger:** What will still prompt you to act? *Example: Feeling stressed after work.*

- **New habit:** What action will you take instead of drinking? *Example: Going for a walk, stretching, or journaling.*

- **New reward:** What positive outcome will the new habit provide? *Example: Feeling calmer, clearing my mind, or having a sense of accomplishment.*

Step 4: Build your action plan

1. What's one small step you can take to make the new habit easier? *Example: Keep a pair of walking shoes by the door.*

2. Who or what can support you in sticking to this change?

Example: A friend to join me on walks or a playlist to enjoy while I'm out.

3. How will you remind yourself to follow through?
Example: Set a daily reminder on my phone.

Log:

Trigger	Old habit	Old reward	New habit	New reward
Example: Feeling stressed	Pouring a glass of wine	Temporary relaxation	Going for a walk	Feeling calm and clear

Additional Tips for Success

- **Start small:** Focus on replacing one habit at a time.

- **Celebrate your wins:** Acknowledge the positive rewards from your new habits.

- **Stay flexible:** Adjust your plan if something isn't working.

By working through this worksheet, you'll gain clarity on your habits and empower yourself to make intentional, lasting changes. Remember, every step forward is progress!

Free Newsletter

Health, longevity and lifestyle tips and advice

Sign up to get the exclusive e-newsletter, sent out every week

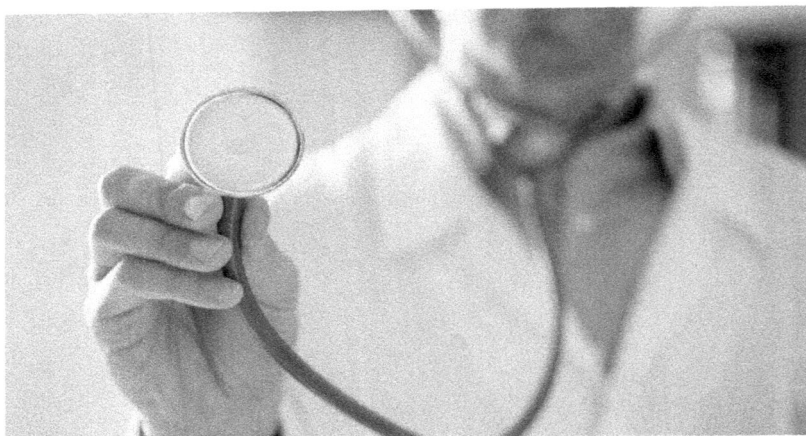

https://www.subscribepage.com/autoimmune

References

Alcohol. (2024, June 28). World Health Organization. https://www.who.int/news-room/fact-sheets/detail/alcohol

Armstrong, L. (2023, April 6). How much is alcohol use really costing you? American Addiction Centers. https://americanaddictioncenters.org/blog/how-much-is-alcohol-use-really-costing-you

Ballard, H. S. (2024). The hematological complications of alcoholism. Alcohol Health and Research World, 21(1), 42. https://pmc.ncbi.nlm.nih.gov/articles/PMC6826798/

Begum, J. (2023). What happens when you quit drinking? WebMD. https://www.webmd.com/mental-health/addiction/ss/slideshow-quit-alcohol-effects

Bishehsari, F., Magno, E., Swanson, G., Desai, V., Voigt, R. M., Forsyth, C. B., & Keshavarzian, A.

(2017). Alcohol and gut-derived inflammation. Alcohol Research: Current Reviews, 38(2), 163. https://pmc.ncbi.nlm.nih.gov/articles/PMC5513683/

Blake, S. (2023, December). How much could you save by giving up alcohol? Newsweek. https://www.newsweek.com/how-much-money-you-save-giving-alcohol-1848804

Bonnie, R. (2015). Alcohol in the media. National Institute of Health; National Academic Press. https://www.ncbi.nlm.nih.gov/books/NBK37586/

Chiasson, D. (2025, January 6). How to conquer cravings during recovery. Casco Bay Recovery. https://cascobayrecovery.com/how-to-conquer-cravings-during-recovery/

Copely, L. (2023, November 30). 30 best journaling prompts for improving mental health. PositivePsychology.com. https://positivepsychology.com/journaling-prompts/

Czepa, C. (2024). How to create a healthy daily routine: Tips for fitness, nutrition, and mental wellness. Live 2 B Healthy. https://live2bhealthy.com/how-to-kickstart-a-healthy-new-routine/

Dresp-Langley, B. (2023, September 1). From reward to anhedonia-dopamine function. Biomedicines. https://doi.org/10.3390/biomedicines11092469

Engels, R. C. M. E., Hermans, R., van Baaren, R. B., Hollenstein, T., & Bot, S. M. (2009). Alcohol portrayal on television affects actual drinking behaviour. Alcohol and Alcoholism, 44(3), 244–249. https://doi.org/10.1093/alcalc/agp003

Fisher, B. (2023, April 26). 10 tips for practicing gratitude in recovery. The Ridge Ohio. https://theridgeohio.com/blog/practicing-gratitude-in-recovery/

https://www.facebook.com/live2bhealthy.

Julius, S. (2024). Benefits that happen when you stop drinking. Townsendla. https://www.townsendla.com/blog/benefits-stop-drinking

Koob, G. F. (2023, September 22). Neuroscience: The brain in addiction and recovery. National Institute on Alcohol Abuse and Alcoholism. https://www.niaaa.nih.gov/health-professionals-communities/core-resource-on-alcohol/neuroscience-brain-addiction-and-recovery

Moreno, M. A., & Whitehill, J. M. (2014). Influence of social media on alcohol use in adolescents and young adults. Alcohol Research. 36(1) 91–100. https://pmc.ncbi.nlm.nih.gov/articles/PMC4432862/

Mosunic, C. (2024, May 28). How to socialize without alcohol. Calm Blog. https://www.calm.com/blog/how-to-socialize-without-alcohol

Merrill, J. E. & Thomas, S. E. (2013, March). Interactions between adaptive coping and drinking to cope in predicting naturalistic drinking and drinking following a lab-based psychosocial stressor. Addictive Behaviors. 38(3) 1672-1678. https://doi.org/10.1016/j.addbeh.2012.10.003

NIH. (2024, September). Alcohol use disorder (AUD): Age groups and demographic characteristics. National Institute on Alcohol Abuse and Alcoholism; National Institute of Health. https://www.niaaa.nih.gov/alcohols-effects-health/alcohol-topics/alcohol-facts-and-statistics/alcohol-use-disorder-aud-united-states-age-groups-and-demographic-characteristics

Rusbatch, S. (2024, June 13). Why setting boundaries is essential in early sobriety. Sarah

Rusbatch Drinking Coach and Speaker.
https://sarahrusbatch.com/blog/why-setting-
boundaries-is-essential-in-early-sobriety-and-how-
to-do-it

Rydzewska, M., Zaorska, J., & Jakubczyk, A.
(2023). The regulation of emotions and
problematic alcohol use: a review of literature.
Alcoholism and Drug Addiction, 36(2).
https://doi.org/10.5114/ain.2023.132441

Sachdev, P. (2023, October 8). What Is alcohol
withdrawal? WebMD.
https://www.webmd.com/mental-
health/addiction/alcohol-withdrawal-symptoms-
treatments

Sadick, B. (2024, February 22). What Happens to
Your Body When You Quit Alcohol for a Month.
AARP. https://www.aarp.org/health/healthy-
living/info-2024/stop-drinking-for-a-month-
benefits.html

Sharp, A. (2024, April 8). Alcohol withdrawal
symptoms, timeline & detox treatment. American
Addiction Centers.
https://americanaddictioncenters.org/alcohol/wit
hdrawal-detox

Sudhinaraset, M., Wigglesworth, C., & Takeuchi,
D. T. (2016). Social and cultural contexts of

alcohol use. Alcohol Research. 38(1) 35–45. https://pmc.ncbi.nlm.nih.gov/articles/PMC4872611/

Sullivan, E. V., Harris, R. A., & Adolf Pfefferbaum. (2024). Alcohol's effects on brain and behavior. Alcohol Research & Health. https://pmc.ncbi.nlm.nih.gov/articles/PMC3625995/

Sutton, J. (2018, May 14). 5 benefits of journaling for mental health. Positive Psychology. https://positivepsychology.com/benefits-of-journaling/

Travers, M. (2024, July 2). A psychologist explains the rising concern around "hangxiety." Forbes. https://www.forbes.com/sites/traversmark/2024/07/02/a-psychologist-explains-the-rising-concern-around-hangxiety/

Trevisan, L. A., Boutros, N., Petrakis, I. L., & Krystal, J. H. (2024). Complications of alcohol withdrawal: Pathophysiological insights. Alcohol Health and Research World, 22(1), 61. https://pmc.ncbi.nlm.nih.gov/articles/PMC6761825/

Wandler, K. (2024, May 3). The positive impacts of quitting alcohol. The Recovery Village Palm Beach.

https://www.floridarehab.com/alcohol/benefits-of-quitting-alcohol/

Vazifehkhorani, K., Attaran, A., Saraskandrud, A., Faghih, H., & Yeganeh, N. (2022). Effectiveness of cue-exposure therapy on alcohol craving and habit loops. Addict Health, 14(2). https://doi.org/10.22122/AHJ.2022.196454.1288

Volkow, N. D., Michaelides, M., & Baler, R. (2019, September 11). The neuroscience of drug reward and addiction. Physiological Reviews. 99(4) 2115-2140. https://doi.org/10.1152/physrev.00014.2018

Ways, R.B. (2024, December 4). How to handle alcohol cravings. Sober Powered. https://www.soberpowered.com/getting-started-blog/how-to-handle-alcohol-cravings